William Stinson Blanchard

The Pilgrims

A poem

William Stinson Blanchard

The Pilgrims
A poem

ISBN/EAN: 9783337289386

Printed in Europe, USA, Canada, Australia, Japan

Cover: Foto ©Thomas Meinert / pixelio.de

More available books at **www.hansebooks.com**

THE PILGRIMS.

A POEM,

BY

REV. PROFESSOR W. S. BLANCHARD,

LATE OF THE CHAIR OF ANCIENT LANGUAGES AND HISTORY,
CLEVELAND UNIVERSITY.

"They despised everything but virtue."
PLATO.

"Men whose life, learning, faith and good intent
Would have been held in high esteem with Paul."
MILTON.

CHICAGO:
PUBLISHED BY GOODSPEED'S EMPIRE PUBLISHING HOUSE,
New York, Cincinnati, New Orleans.
1872.

PREFACE.

The author owes the public a brief apology, perhaps.
for allowing the following Poem, rapidly written, without
Horace's " limæ labor et mora," to appear before the world.
Having been solicited by a friend, in whose judgment he
confides, to prepare an ode suitable to be used on acca-
sion of the public celebration of the two hundred and
fiftieth anniversary of the landing at Plymouth,— thrown
thereby into a meditative mood, on the disinterestedness,
grandeur and moral sublimity of the undertaking of the Pilgrims—so full of germ seeds, vast results in revolutionary
aggrandizement to nations, quickening the entire race of
man—he has prosecuted their praise still farther. Without
thought of courting the muse, or seeking literary reputa-
tion, but with profound impression of the value of the
services the Pilgrims have rendered society, it is offered
as an humble tribute to their memory. Whatever imperfec-
tions it may contain,—and none can be more conscious
than the author himself that they are manifold, and
which, had time made it practicable, should have been

greatly chastised,—such as it is, claiming nothing save honest intention in contributing somewhat to the memory of the lives and deeds of the grandest heroic men the ages have produced, the author sends it forth, asking God's blessing upon it.   He does so, moreover, the more readily from the conviction that the taste of the multitude, too ready to nauseate at sterling excellencies and virtues, feeds on the trashy and barren nonsense of unhealthy and exciting fictions, the conjuration of heated fancies stimulated by avaricious motives.   In originalities, self-abnegation, renunciation, grand heroisms of thrilling adventures, matchless triumphs, the Pilgrims annihilate fiction, yea, turn what might be looked upon as impossible fiction into stupendous realities, whose contemplation can but profit, as they themselves are worthy of the constant and reverent regard of a grateful posterity.   W. S. B.

CHICAGO, July, 1872.

THE PILGRIMS.

PART I.

The centuries roll,—their flowers bloom,
O'er wreck and ruin waft perfume,
Vast policies of light ordain,
Crush tyrant rule, by freedom's reign !
Two hundred fifty years ago,
In exile, poverty and woe,
Far o'er the tempest curtained sea
Came the great Sires of Liberty,
The Pilgrim band, whose hero fame
Stars now great centuries with their name,—
Through sacrifice, through faith sublime,
Foremost in all the ranks of time !
Herculean sires, of princely mould,
Grand liberators,—Heaven enrolled,—

Light of the ages yet to be,—
Immortal champions of the Free!
Their mission Truth, they plant a world,
New, glorious ensigns high unfurl'd,
Wave their bright folds of radiant light,
Before which error sinks in night!
With conquering skill, resistless power,
They deep illume Time's ill-starr'd hour,
Bequeath new heir-loom to mankind,
Earth's galling fetters, chains unbind,
With giant force wide strew the ground
With heaviest yokes blind custom bound,
The cause of Justice man proclaim,
Put tyrants to eternal shame!
With high, resplendent, glorious thought,
Germs with imperial harvests fraught,
Darting swift gleams of heavenly fire,
Whose leavening mould lifts nations higher,
Whose kindling glories, purging ray,
Chase spectral darkness, glooms away,
They, of the ages great, supreme,
Enlight the earth with central beam
Of Love's soft, genial, blissful power,
Its temples deck with fadeless flower,

Heaven's worship consecrate anew
'Mid falling, light, sweet, pearly dew;
Fore-tasting joys, whose springs e'er rise
In balmier, lovelier, brighter skies!
Intent in duty's path to tread,
On heavenly manna nectar-fed,
Th' arch-fiend, 'mid his satanic spell,
They battle, kindling fires of hell,
Forestall the doom of mortal death,
For God, mankind consume their breath!
Immortal guides, their virtues strong,
Their deeds time's grandest epic song!
Rebuke of ages passed away,
In schemes ill-judged, worm'd with decay,
They light new altars e'er to burn;
On axle new the centuries turn;
The dismal waters, dark and drear,
Touched by their wand, grown crystal clear!
In their own land defamed, unknown,
They firm uphold monarchic throne,
•Stud England's brow, queen of the sea,
With radiant gems of Liberty;
'Mid deep convulsions, strife and storm,
Fearless they rush, with bosoms warm,

Their country's honor proud to save,
For that oft find a martyr grave!
Like heroes of the olden time,
Whose deathless deeds the centuries chime,
They prowess, valor's charms inspire,
Quicken a world with new desire;
Dark tyrant hosts give battle, scorn,
Herald proud Freedom's hastening morn;
Its sacred advent, laws divine,
Grand, spotless policies that shine,
Glancing bright beams 'long golden hills,
While earth with radiance sunshine fills;
Cause a new flame beneath the sun
To burst and through time's stubble run;
Pour deepening splendors far and wide,
Make man, God's child, the ages, pride!
Fired with immortal, quenchless zeal,
Time's vast pulsations through them steal;
Deep stirred with sentiments profound,
They long, they pant for hallowed ground,
With prophet ken, visions ablaze,
Wrapt in a dream of future days,
'Mid the huge structures power had built,
For which vast seas of blood were spilt,

Limn'd on their view a kingdom bright,—
Beauteous in bloom,—vast realm of Right,
Where all unscourged, erect and free,
Man to his Maker bows the knee!
Heaven's gracious boon, tow'ring sublime
Beyond these darkening scenes of time,
A nearing form of grandeur true,
Flashing the sunlight centuries through,
'Mid whose unclouded, spotless day
Mankind shall pass from wrongs away!
Sweet form great Titans might inspire,
Rouse lethargy with quenchless fire,
Each meditative soul expand,
Panting for God's bright, better land!
For that imperial, crowning prize,
Each moment charged as swift it flies,
Ceaseless they toil, oft smile and weep,
Achieve grand triumphs, vigils keep;
Burst the vile bars that hem them round,
Suffer, resolve, toil, plan profound,
Till vexed by land, by surging sea,
In struggles vain for Liberty,
They sink desponding, sad, oppress'd,
No land to give their footsteps rest:

Like wearied birds, when from their seat
Fierce tempests drive, unpitying beat,
With plaintive airs sad fate will mourn,
Their beauteous plumage drench'd and torn;
They, the proud champions of a world,
Are by tyrannic vengeance hurled,
Toss'd, shaken, riven, bruis'd, plunder'd, peal'd,
Their fortunes dubious, darkly sealed;
No auguring omens lighting near;
No visions soothe their falling tear;
No voice oracular can hear!
At length Heaven's awful summons rang,
When past the dreadful parting pang;
The nation's hope, the purged, refined,
Most glorious gifted of mankind,
Earth's galling chains ordained to break,
Vast realm of glory yet to make;
New trials on their vision crowd:
An unknown deep, death's watery shroud,
Disseverance from human life,
To plunge in nature's giant strife;
Vast thickening ills, no sunbeam ray
Falling athwart their Pilgrim way!
For them the path to Heavenly bliss

Lay through the deep, vast wilderness,
Where lions roar, where monsters roam,
Driven from their country, native home;
Terrific vengeance, land and sea,
Threatening their tempted destiny!
But waves that rise, that dismal roll,
No portents dire unman their soul;
In sweet composure, purpose grand,
They seek the Heaven appointed land;
Their path no mortal footsteps trod,
None saw them save their guardian God;
Perils behind, perils before,
They seek an unknown savage shore,
A land, to Fancy's boding eye,
Where blood-smeared chiefs insult, defy,
Of war-whoops, wailing, bloody dance,
Dread tomahawk, vile spear and lance,
Of cruel rites, orgies of blood,
Whose spectral terrors haunt the flood!
Dark land! no civic germs had burst,
Of rock-bound shores, enlocked in frost;
Where darkness since the reign of time
Had reigned supreme, in power sublime;
Its awful silence all unbroke,

Save when the savage war-chief spoke!
Dread wilderness of vast expanse,
Whose warring tribes forbade advance;
Whose solitude, no tongue could tell
What drama-dirges there did swell,—
What beacon lights had there been fired
While empires rose, triumph'd, expired!
Yet, while beset by dismal foes,
While mightiest obstacles oppose,
Such as would make firm hearts of steel
Blush, trepidate, all dubious feel,
No murmuring sigh, desponding fear,
With weakness dims their high career,
Palsies their arm, pales their staunch brow,
Stagnates their life-tide's crimsoning flow,
Unnerves their zeal, cools, drives them back
On their o'er-passed, wave-crested track;
With souls of fire, with hearts of flame,
Across the surging deep they came,
Bearing high Heaven's inviolable trust,—
The noble, brave, the virtuous, just,
To Truth,—Religion,—Freedom, dear,
They consecrate a Hemisphere!
This western world make Pilgrim land,

A glorious beacon, peerless, grand !
New Palestina, where the race,
Long peel'd, oppress'd, finds sheltering place !
Say, mighty muse, what humble lays
Shall yield them worthy, fitting praise ?
Who Jason-like to Colchis bound,
Here more than golden-fleece have found,—
Who like Ulysses, wandering, driven,
Beneath the glittering dome of heaven,
O'er wrathful seas in ceaseless rage,
Where elements fierce battle wage,—
Here mightiest labors cause to end,
Power, letters, law, truth, art, extend !
O muse, proud of thy halo's gleam,
Their brow deep trace with Glory's beam ;
Lift their unspotted name on high,
To live when suns, when stars shall die !
Be thou inspired, the numbers fill,—
Bid, bid Castalia's dews distill ;
Bind thou the laurel, garland twine ;
Th' immortal honor shall be thine !
Nor time, nor age shall dim that fame,
Enshrined by Glory's deepening flame !
Humbly they came, no pageants sound,

Stir the vast world, creation round,
Startle the nations, give unrest,
Hungering for lands, yet unpossessed !
Silent, unknown, they launch away;
No admiral's pennants round them play,
Power, its protection comes not nigh,—
Alone to live, alone to die;
Though worthy, 'mid the heaving main
Of escort, an imperial train,
No royal smiles cheer the long way
To where new El Dorados lay;
No greeting looks of neighbor, friend,
Of loved ones, consolation lend;
No magic ties, friendship's fond smile,
For them the tedious hours beguile.
Sweet thoughts of home, of childhood's day,
A vanished dream, fled far away :—
The waste, dark, boundless, heaving sea,
Waters whose voice is destiny,
Vast, all inscrutable, profound,—
They wall their azure dome around !
No dazzling baits of empire grand,
Bright glittering gold in untrod land,—
Pearls, diamonds, rubies, priceless gems,

Stars, garters, ribbons, diadems,—
Escutcheon'd grandeur, Glory, Fame,
Hereditary titles, name,—
Earth's sordid boon,—ambition's prize,—
Seeking grand conquests 'neath all skies,—
Fire their meek souls with proud desire.
To kindle here God's altar-fire!
'Twas the dread hour of tyrant wrath;
Its damning edicts cross their path,
Its heavy curses heaped their head;
Fierce lightnings, earthquake, where they tread,
Dark riving bolts in terror sped;
E'en ocean, its dark watery bed,
Sweet blessings to the woes they dread!
Oppression in relentless form,
The avalanche, the bursting storm,
Huge, sunless terror of a world
In ruin's blackening vortex whirled,
Unveiled, through centuries dire and long,
Time's crushing heritage of wrong;
Th' avenging ghosts of slaughtering Power
Shrieking its curse from shore to shore;
Telling a world of guilt and crime,
Dread, foul obliquities of Time!

Thick deepening folds of darkness lay
On mightiest realms,—no star of day,—
While man to Heaven in vain still cried,
At morn, at noon, at even-tide,
How long! O Lord, Great, Just and True,
Wilt thou not break man's pathway through?
Rend from th' embondaged, bleeding race
Each iron yoke of foul disgrace,—
Dread scourge of sovereign despot power
With thine own vengeance burn, devour,—
Lift on man's longing, anxious sight
Some banner traced with changeless Right,—
By thy victorious guiding hand
Thy servants show the promised land,—
End of these ills, these thickening woes,—
Lead where the crystal water flows,
Where Freedom, Truth, in triumph reign,
Nor man of bondage more complain?
On midnight skies a twilight gleamed·—
Tho't sparkled, flashed,—in radiance gleamed—
Hope fled, revived, bright signals streamed.
Peradventure grew, as certain seemed,
On Europe's soil, there broke no ray,
Of brighter civil, moral day;

No harps' sweet echoes in the blast
Presage deliverances at last,—
No trumpets' clangor's crashing sound
Fires earth's great hosts, the lands around,
To hurl swift thunderbolts afar,
And crown the centuries' ceaseless war !
Dark, dismal, grew the fate of man ;
No patriot heroes in the van,
Their fearful falchions waving high,
Fearless to do, to dare, and die ;
With an Herculean arm of might
Crown victory with eternal Right,
Maintain just, righteous, equal power,
Dissolve the threatening mists that lower,
Solve the great problems, deep, divine,
Round unborn ages garlands twine !
Trembling, impassioned, in their grief,
Whence, whence, they ask, shall come relief,—
What mighty messengers of God
Shall smite the sea with prophet rod,—
Amid the long, deep draughts of woe,
For man, who bid the nectar flow,—
Make his proud consciousness to swell
'Neath Freedom's live-long magic spell,

Send its blest voices, happier strain,
O'er continents, o'er bounding main ;
Give to the blast its clarion sound,
To break triumphant earth around !
What unknown remedies appear,
Staunch earth's long woe, dry falling tear,
Tear from man's back proscription's load,
Lead human nature up to God !
All human spheres convulsive driven,
From center to circumference riven.
High, low, all ranks in error whelm'd,
Chaotic policies condemned,
Proud wisdom palled in gloom of night,
Selectest reason void of light,—
From what mysterious change, high power,
Shall fall the sunshine on the hour,
Dissolving beams of radiance pour,
Flood the dark world, from door to door ;
Its hoary bondage melt away
'Mid opening gates of new-born day ;
The midnight sorrows of the past,
Adown oblivion's steep be cast ;
The mountain load of brutal Might
Crumble before eternal Right !

'Mid deepening praises loud and long,
The triumph tones of Time's great song,
The nations swelling each grand peal,
Each despot's, tyrant's doom to seal!
Whence come the fiat loud and long,
Shivering the blood-stain'd throne of Wrong!
What glorious cause, proud, high command,
Bid and be heard to farthest land,
Unnumbered blessings ceaseless flow,
Through Time, to all the centuries go,
Earth's grandest destinies unfold,
There dawn prophetic age of gold,
Unshackled, laurel'd, brave and free,
Man walk erect in Liberty;
His powers, himself, all, all his own,
Mightier than monarch on the throne!
Long in despondency, deep gloom,
Dark, thickening clouds presaging doom,
No dial hand to point the time,
Insuring changes grand, sublime;
New trophies, conquests, victories dear,
Re-modeling empires, hemisphere;
Roused by vast thoughts, their quickening fire
Burns, kindles their Heaven-born desire,

To act some noble, generous part,
On higher plane of life to start;
The generations,—deck their place,
Ascending,—in high Glory's race ;—
To be meek almoners of good,
New structures rear, for man, for God,
Open new pathways, bright to shine,
Flooding with beams of truth divine !
Amid the tossings of the deep,
Where mountain billows pile and sweep,
They, a grand Future, glorious, see,
Progress, Grandeur, true Liberty ;—
Magnificence, Resplendence, Fame,—
Triumphs that clothe the past with shame !
As in a dream, the soul will wake,
Of high enrapturing bliss partake,
A land they glimpse, all lovely, fair,
In answer to their midnight prayer ;
Grand prize, glories immortal, rare,
Hush their forebodings, soothes their care ;—
Sweet land of refuge, peace and love,
Gushing with founts from realms above,
Mind darkened by no galling chain,
Where tyrants ne'er usurp nor reign,

Where principles eternal bloom,
Where sweetest incense wafts perfume ;—
Law, sovereign from the seat of God,
High paths of Virtue, Glory, trod ;—
Statesmen, proud patriots, all aflame,
Starring with Right immortal name;
Truth, Justice, Freedom, laurel'd dear,
Life's sweetened waters crystal clear ;—
Ambition's lust, kindling false zeal,
No happy spirit doomed to feel;
Pure social joys by all possessed,—
Sweet land by vices unoppressed !—
Blest fount of knowledge opened wide,
Eternal wisdom, Teacher, Guide !
Man's safety, sovereign welfare, planned,
On adamantine base to stand,—
All that can rouse, move, warm, desire,
Kindle the deep Promethean fire,
Towers on their sight, in visions blest,—
Sweet land of promise, land of rest !
They gaze, see buds, fair glorious fruit,
Shoot, flower, on Heaven's prolific root ;
Light breaks around, deep, strong, intense,
That thrills, enraptures inmost sense,

Drops from each bough, each emerald leaf,
Decks purple bud, each golden sheaf ;—
Prophetic harmonies increase,
Sweet choiring tell that strifes must cease,
Dread carnage, war, soon, soon be o'er,
Prosperities crown every shore,—
Sweet blushing verdure, mantling green,
Gemm'd with bright flowers, by all be seen ;
Dark reign of guilt, of woe be past,
'Mid brightening splendors falling fast !
Unearthly ministries appear,—
They seem embarked on upper sphere,
Mysterious airs, superior mien,
Them the great stormy deep between,
Earth's labors, pastimes, callings, love,
Transfiguring as in realms above ;—
Beings all spiritual, grand, sublime,
Throng the bright picturing veils of Time,
Pressing in myriad numbers bright,
Purging their dross, proud sons of Light !
Life 'reft of fear, hope firm, secure ;
Vast banner'd hosts, bright, spotless, pure,
Guarding, impregnable, and strong,
Rolling great freedom's airs along ;—

All dark mementos passed away,
Oblivious, lost 'mid brightening day!
As from a trance, prophetic spell,
They wake, hear the loud thundering swell
Of ocean, awful, dread, sublime,
Voices as from some happier clime,
Break on their ear, uplift each soul,
In diapasons—musical,—
Voices beyond the bounding sea,
Like accents from eternity,
Telling that man shall yet be free,
His birthright, God-given Liberty!
Vouchsafed such visions 'mid their toil,
While tyrants rage, darken, despoil,—
Tossed by the deep, on mission grand,
May they not find some beauteous land,
More lovely than the lands that are,
Plant Sharon's rose, sweet lilies there,
Fair flowers unfailing in their bloom,
To shed a ceaseless, rich perfume;
A land to them of genial power,
Where they may spend allotted hour;
Lay strong foundations, broad and deep,
'Gainst which in vain Time's waves shall
    sweep;

Deck, grace, adorn with Beauty's smile,
With thymy pastures, sylvan wile ;
With shading bowers, where at each morn
Shall wind abundance' cheering horn ;—
There, where blest Freedom's flashing wave
Shall grandly roll the earth to lave ;
Where its grand mission proud shall start,
Rear column'd shrines of glorious art ;
Vast towers to pierce heaven's boundless blue,
To stand long coming ages through ;
On whose proud summit light shall play
When they from earth have passed away !
Stamp the pure rock of deathless mind ;
With their own virtues chaste, refined,
Wake hungerings for immortal food,
Pure, mental, moral, spiritual Good ;
Give to the world Time's grandest prize,
Freedom's great flame that never dies !
A flame that travels nor retires ;
That lights proud Glory's beacon fires,
Flashing its beams the centuries through ;
Building mankind the world anew ;—
In whose effulgence high o'er-spann'd ;
Times' crowning structures roseate stand

Lo ! from the Past, 'tis Heaven-enscrolled ;
God takes his servants from the fold,
When He by miracle would trace
A brightning pathway for the race ;
Give Law-Giver to ages wide,—
Great Bard, sweet-tongued, Siloa's pride ;
His people smit by tyrant hand,
Driven in exile from their land;
Through stormy seas, through perils dire,
He brings to kindle Zion's fire ;—
Rear the vast temple famed of old,
Whose pillar'd dome, vast sea of gold,
Flashed beams symbolic of Heaven's love,
Redemption's hieroglyph from above ;—
Vast prophecy of ending night,
Scaffolding Him who was the Light!
God's heroes in Time's drama-play,
Proud Pilgrims on the world's highway,—
Part of th' illustrious, glorious band,
Heaven-chosen, sent on mission grand ;
May they not plant some mighty land,
With Glory's arch to be o'er-spanned,
Streams flow with nectar from their hand,
Quench man's long thirst by God's command !

Scanning Heaven's high, august decree,
They hunger, pant, all flesh to free ;
Bind in new ties of union sweet
The countless millions time shall greet,
Fire man's proud soul, immortal mind,
With mightiest themes, all chains unbind ;
By cultured thought, by taste profound,
Fling bright Perfection's charms around ;
Light the dark world from side to side,
Give civilizations healthful stride,
Lop foul excrescences, repair
All drooping excellencies rare ;
Retone, shape, build a convulsed world,
Dashed, shaken, downward, upward whirled !
Haste on predicted age of power ;
When o'er the lands 'long every shore
Vast seas of splendor, light shall roll,
From center to the utmost pole ;
When through bright gates of sapphire, pearl,
Love's starry banners shall unfurl,
Apocalypse of woe be sealed,
Millennial brightness shine revealed
O'er all the earth,—purged of its guilt ;
No more vast seas of blood be spilt ;

The world no more in bondage, shame,
Lit by ambition's maddening flame ;
But Paradise of joy, of peace,
Where wrongs redressed forever cease,
Loud thundering songs of jubilee,
Bursting from myriad myriads Free !
From out the ages grand and long,
Great hero souls in valor strong ;
God's chosen ones, Heaven's quenchless fire,
Deep-burning kindles vast desire ;
They labor, suffer, toil, aspire,
Pant for a coming age of Light ;
Pure, Heavenly-featured, radiant, bright,
Stuck o'er with no dark things of clay,
The rubbish, dross, dissolved away,
'Mid breaking beams of Heavenly Truth,
Deepening its charms, perennial youth ;—
They fill with honest hero pride,
To see vice baffled, turned aside ;
Virtue e'er hail immortal prize ;
Inwove with Freedom's destinies ;—
Seek human happiness, man's peace,
Wealth, Fortune, Glory, ne'er to cease ;
All grandest lineaments of power,

With excellence earth, Time endower !
They, the dark world's unworthy great ;
See, soulless tyrants, scorn, and hate,—
On Heaven's high list of Fame enrolled,
See them for barter vilely sold !
Wearing Heaven's spotless robe of white,
In spiritual traceries trophies bright,—
Helmed by vast power, unseen and rare,
Omnipotence, its guardian care ;
Stemming the awful waves of Time ;
Towering in character sublime ! ´
By dreadest foes scoffed, vilified,
Hunted the world from side to side,—
The ages grandest living pride,
On sorrows dark and stormy tide,
Driven tempestuous far and wide ;—
No falling splendors from the sun,
Darkness, the path left them to run !
O mystery ! is such the road
All travel, who for man, for God,
Would leave proud testimonies rare,
Light, Glory, Power, to ages bear !
Sublime its Greatness,—man beware,—
Tis won through agonies, despair !

Heaven gives but few that gift to know,
The grandest boon God can bestow
On mortal man,—selectest prize,—
His fellow man to peer, outrise;
Be endless ranked among the wise,
Who beacons earth, to Glory hies;
Hymn'd by the Beatific throng
Of Martyrs in eternal song !
Who, who can tell till trial's doom,
Give bright experience, conquering plume.
Who firm can stand the test, ordeal,
That greatness makes immortal, real ?
Who, till temptation's hour of strife,
From shadow, brings true Substance, Life,
Revealing spirit, conscience, soul,
Reason, its Mastery, self-control ?
When hoary wrong would bind the chain
On rectitude, its course restrain,
Hush conscience' voice, menacing pain,
That Error empire dark may gain;
He who amid the wrong's assay,
Can spurn all lures, fling bold away
Each vicious bait,—he, he can be
The truly great, heroic, free ;

And he alone, who else would rise,
Grows infamous, forgotten dies,—
His name, his fame, posterity,
Beclouded with black infamy!
Not thus the Pilgrims, whom we sing,
Whose praise shall through all ages ring
In deepening tones, inspiring prayer,
Telling the lands, Lo! faith was there!
Gaping with wounds, in trickling gore,
Time waxing darker evermore;
Oppressed, crushed, doomed, by native land,
Its glory set, once radiant, grand,
Kindling with flames from Heaven above,
Fired with vast quenchless thoughts of Love,
Rejected, scorned, they bound away,
Magnanimous, to find new way
For man to empire, power and fame,
Inheritance, immortal name;—
With new discoveries garland Time,
Deck earth with grandest deeds sublime!
While thoughts of blessing rule their breast,
See them by calumnies oppress'd,
With foul aspersions covered o'er;
Distance enchantment found no more,

Behind fierce wrath, sorrows before ;
Yet, see how gloriously they rise,
All groveling lures, foul tests dspise ;
Bent on grand mission for a world ;
Faith their true shield, Truth's flag unfurl'd,
Outraged, imprisoned, fettered, bound,
They seek a home on hallowed ground ;—
A safe retreat from cruel wrong,
Where they may lift Love's grateful song !
Blackness of darkness round them hung,
Their hearts with deepest anguish wrung ;
Though visions blest burst on their eyes,
Hope's beam oft quenched 'mid midnight skies,
Scouting all omens perils drear,
Pondering the world for them to steer,
Heaven's Pilgrim band, driven ocean o'er,
Safe guided to their destined shore,
While long the way outstretch'd still lies
No land yet bursting on their eyes,
No auspice whispering their relief,
Surcharged with unassuaged grief ;
Votaries of prayer, they ask Heaven light,—
Ends, ends their dreary, starless night !
Duty's great path now clears, grows bright ;

God's word, their conscience in the right,
Visions of glory give delight !
Great laurel'd champions, pure, upright,
Whom perils, dangers, ne'er affright ;
For whom Heaven's Zodiac moves aright ;
Humble, trustful, repentant, trite ;
Heroes of grand Herculean might,
Stern foes of war's dark, bloody fight,
Seeking for empire grander site ;
Earth's millions here to lure, invite,
In holier ties and bonds unite ;
Man find from tyranny respite,
Scale Truth's great flaming mountain height,
Chased by no wizard sickly sprite ;
'Mid paling shades of brief twilight,
From Honor's path ne'er put to flight,
With span but as of yester-night ;
Yet endless destinies to write,
In beam of Heaven's purged, stainless white,
While obstacles still Hope would fright ;
While Fancy's specters down alight;
While slander spotless names would blight ;
Seeking all hell to rouse, incite,
Which God's dread vengeance yet shall smite ;

Remorse devour with scorpion bite,
Crush with a grasp than death more tight;
The fiendish demon without rite,—
Careering to their goal despite;
They sigh no more their doleful plight,
But give the ages grandest sight!
Time's unread grandees, magnates, brave,
Commissioned hopes forlorn to save;
To blazon Fame on architrave,
Beyond the ocean's rolling wave;
They, their great trust, now conscious, feel;
Labors would end, their mission seal
With Glory's triumph, Glory's palm,—
Complete the music of Life's psalm!
Wasted by woes, consumed by fears,
Fleeting unblest their mortal years;
Their energies, great powers unspent,
Heaven for sublimest action lent;
To aid, advance Truth's mighty cause;
Virtue, wise order, Equal Laws,
Move the vast world, to ills consigned,
By holier policies refined;
Pour fadeless splendor on Time's hour;
Re-orb its damaged, shattered power;

Build for the ages structures grand,
Unknown before in any land!
On, on, their course they valiant keep,
Scanning the omens of the deep;
Lo! the great path of Destiny
Opens beyond th' untraveled sea,
'Mid lands remote, tenantless still,
Long veiled by Heaven's ordaining will,
Where, as grand influences distil,
Time's destinies re-orb, fulfil.
Thither, thro' gloom, Faith points the way
To empire grand, of boundless sway,
Where Christ's pure church, the Civil State,
Crushed, bleeding, torn, may re-create
On sure foundations; pillars raise
'Mid flooding splendors, purging rays
Of Heavenly light; grow strong, secure,
Thro' nameless ages firm endure.
God's pilgrim host from o'er the deep
Here they may guardian vigils keep,
Long, long as Time's great course is sped,
In independence lift their head,
Earth's glorious sons to Freedom true,

Unthralled, unstigmatized, anew,
Man's changing fortunes, fate review,
New destinies, high hopes pursue,
Relight the world's extinguished fires,
Before which Darkness, driven, expires,
And live great hero Pilgrim sires !
Martyrs of Truth, champions of Right,—
They brave the gloom of moral night;
Brave the vast ocean, all untrod,—
For freedom here to worship God !
They come,—Time's grandest blessings bring,
The forests smile, the dim woods ring,
Unwonted echoes break around,
Creation gladdens at the sound;
Th' unbroken centuries' shadows flee,
Wakes Nature's grandest minstrelsy,
Vast mountain summits, plains untrod,
Welcome the messengers of God ;
The hills from their deep granite bed
Rush, 'round the Mayflower lift their head,
Break the dark ocean's smiting staff,
Whose billows lull, in concert laugh ;
The elements in choral song
Roll their great harmonies along;

Earth, air, the sea, the vaulted sky,
Shout wondrous joy, make glad reply,
As that immortal Pilgrim band
Bow in meek reverence 'long the strand!
Drips with bright radiance Freedom's star,
Sweet, purple gates of morn unbar,
Flash with intense, deep, golden ray,
Drive century wrongs dissolved away;
Light breaks, of deep'ning, glorious beam,
Transcendant, soon to grow supreme;—
Light such as ne'er from conqueror streamed,
From proud ambition never gleamed,
The light of Hope, not of Dismay,
Sweet dawning beams of bright'ning day
To pierce all lands, each starless deep,
Break the vast world's unconscious sleep,
Bearing to man in bondage, cheer,
Pure streams of joy, bright, crystal, clear;
End to his woe, deliverance near!
Then pealed the mightiest bell of Time,
Rang then the century's grandest chime,
Heard thro' all lands, by high, renowned,
Piercing the tomb's dark, sacred ground,
Tyrants, deep dozing, unaware

Of empires crumbling 'neath their care ;—
Extinguished altars blaze and burn,
In shrouds of dust, great heroes turn,
Expanding power in sweet surprise,
Sees the great martyr spirits rise,
From every land, who toiled and bled,
In glory lift their laureled head;
The glorious great, to Fancy dear,
In sympathy through every sphere,
They, the exalted, brave, refined,
Break long repose, proud garlands bind!—
E'en generous Greece, with classic dust,
O'er hill, through vale, her cerements burst :
Heroes at Marathon, who fell,
Feel the vast throb, the world-wide spell ;
They, who proud Rome's great eagles saw,
Who once gave empire, equal law;
The noble, just, of every age,
Who star Time's proud recording page,
They wake, they rise, immortal throng,
Pour shout of triumph over Wrong ;
Marshaled in one vast bright'ning train,
They cast fond glance beyond the main,
Pour blessings on the Pilgrim's head,

Then sink and sleep in Glory's bed !
Great voices fall along the sky,
The great intelligencies high
Descend, shout back their grand reply,
E'en as at great Messiah's birth,
Who then proclaimed Truth's reign on earth !
They come,—but not as others came,—
To desolate with fire and flame,—
For mirth,—vain pomp,—proud revelry,—
For feats of arms,—high chivalry,—
They come for Honor's crowning prize,—
A diadem that never dies ;—
To build for virtue's starry train,
Vast empire o'er Atlantic main ;
By policies of righteous law,
Nations in grand allegiance draw :
Cast earth's oppressors, tyrants down,
Lift prostrate Right, star just Renown ;
Here as the forest-aisles shall ring
With anthems loud, to Heaven's high King,
Man stamped with an immortal dye,
May lift his beaming forehead high ;
Rouse patriotism's slumbering fire,
Freedom's vast hosts new nerve, inspire,

With glittering, radiant, crowning crest,
Give succor, aid, to earth's oppress'd,
In human nature's sunless hour,
Crushed bleeding Truth uphold, empower;
In each great battle strife of wrong
Roll Right's triumphant claims along;
Speak to a panic-sticken world,
In ruins awful vortex whirled,
Till from devouring waves forlorn,
From darkness, death, Life, Power, are born;—
Freed from blind follies, fraud and crime,
With undertakings vast, sublime,
Carve new, imperial, matchless fame,
To future ages waft a name!
They come to act for man high part,
His mind transform, renew his heart;
His blighted heritage restore,
New tides of Life, of blessing pour;—
Whether 'mid nature's solitude,
A savage in his wigwam rude,
Or Scythian, on his dreary hills,
Where northern blast with vengeance fills,
Or Calmuc, or fierce Tartar host,
Wild Laplander, 'mid endless frost;

Brave, proud Caucassian, nerved with might,
Or Afric's sons, long spoiled of Right,—
Where'er proud man might lift his form,
'Mid sunshine or avenging storm,
Made in the image of his God,
There bid him walk erect, abroad;
Assert his right, his sovereign claim,—
No child of base befouling shame;
With powers unknown, tyrants beware
Of energies that slumber there!
Allied to spirits great and wise
The just enthroned beyond the skies,
Waxing in Strength, in Glory, might,
Peering great dazzling sons of Light!
They come, man's brow with garlands twine
From Truth's unfathomed sparkling mine,
Touch his proud reason's smouldering fire,
Kindle immortal, pure desire,
Rouse the deep instincts of the soul,
Lead to the grandest self-control,
Wake sympathies of spotless aim,
Affinities earth cannot claim
Devotion's zeal, Love's spotless flame;
Conscience, vicegerent of Heaven's law,

Make angel-bright, with no dark flaw;
Omnipotent, man earth to draw,
To virtue's paths, proud, quick disdain
Of tricksome error's luring reign:
A giant power, collossal, strong,
Herculean 'gainst mightiest Wrong,
Relentless tyrant, dark, unfeared,
Truth, its behests obeyed, revered,
Than life itself more loved, endeared!
Stern Duty demi-god to man,
In each great hour to lead the van;—
While man's immortal fires shall burn,
He Heaven's high mandates ne'er to spurn ;—
To buckle on Truth's armor bright,
Go forth in every cause of Right,
'Neath Heaven's protective radiant shield,
Taught by its sovereign will revealed,—
For Honor, Glory, spotless Fame,
In God's, Religion's sacred name;
Dare deeds of Glory, Power sublime,
New footprints make on sands of Time!
They come 'mid perils, dark dismay,
From ages bear the palm away ;
The world's long frenzied maddened gaze,

Charm with bright Truth's ebullient rays,
With deepening mental, moral force,
Renew, enrich Time's ancient course ;—
Cause new orbed splendors bright to burn,
Man's sinful race Heavenward to turn;
New streams of goodness, blessing, flow,
Knowledge divine to centuries go;
Man's Eden deck with radiant bloom,
With endless life enstar the tomb,
Wait for the mystery, slumbering dust,
A Phœnix-angel soon to burst,
'Mid flaming worlds soar swift away,
Pass portals of unending day,
Rise radiant, eternal shine,
Quickening with energies divine;
This life but germ of that to be,
Man's triumph, God's eternity!
Say, hath the muse o'er-stepped just bound,
False meteor light flared wild around,
Sought Fancy's evanescent praise,
The exile wanderers' fame to raise,
Unreal importance, meanings grand,
Given things foundationless to stand?
Lo! what events crowd Time's vast way

Since that far-famed, immortal day
When Mayflower moored within the bay,
Where Plymouth's waters crest and play;
The ice-bound, rock-ribbed, savage coast
Transforms, vast realm, in grandeur lost!
Along the shore, the wintry main,
Breaks now proud Freedom's swelling strain;
Blank Nature waves her genial horn,
Abundance smiles, Beauty is born;
Dark Poverty, with haggard brow,
And deep-scarred Want, no menace now;
Dismaying ills, that come in storm,
Bow giant strength,—the stalwart form,—
With mission dire, have passed away,
And bright'ning fields in sunlight lay!
Where late the savage wigwam rose,
The lily smiles, fresh blooms the rose;
A matchless empire lifts its head
From out the ocean's watery bed,
Whose massive columns pile, and rise,
To where Pacific's murmur dies;
In arts, in arms, fame, unsurpassed,
Time's noblest triumph, grandest, last!
Great beacon-flame of tow'ring light,

Where ne'er shall come dread tyrant Night,
The scourge of power, its curse to bear,
Omen'd with terror, black despair!
See, the bright vision blest fulfilled,
The light prophetic that distilled,
Heralding fortunes, glories rare,
Grand fruits Elysian, Time shall bear!
The mountain tops, they break with day
From valleys broad, now pass away
The dimming mists, deep shadows strong
Hiding the centuries' damning wrong,
'Mid proud, grand, elemental strife,
The Pilgrims search for freedom, life;
The world grows purer in its clime,
Break grander destinies of Time,
Unbind the heavy burdens borne,
Fall, fall the chains through ages worn,
Compassion, friendship, dart new beam,
New hope-lights dawn, in brilliance stream;
Uncertain Fate, foreboding Doubt,
No longer wall true solace out;
Progress, ameliorations, charm
Insure against disaster, harm.
Like Israel, Heaven's favored host,

Journeying dark wilderness acrost,
Foe, horse and rider, whelmed and lost,
His chariots broken 'mid the deep,
While Red-sea waves re-pile and sweep;
God's pillar of fire still guides the way,
Dispels the spectres, Gloom, Dismay,
'Mid radiant light o'er-arched they tread,
By miracle the chosen fed!
Thus the great Pilgrims, Heaven's proud band,
Ordained the founders of this land,—
They o'er dark elements prevail,
Satanic kingdoms vile assail,
Arch whelps of sin, of mischiefs, shame,
Through mighty Faith enstar their name!
By Faith illumined, guided, led,
True heroes brave, they lift their head,
Open great pathway for mankind,
In Heaven's eternal plan divined!
O Muse, while breaks the deep'ning light,
While clouds dissolve of primal night,
While new-born wonders greet all eyes,
Startle, amaze, with grand surprise,
The Pilgrims voyaging, teach, declare,
The mighty fruitage they shall bear,

The mighty monuments they raise,—
What flashing beams enlight their ways;
Rare charms of progress steal amain,
From the long past comes sweet refrain,
Grand songs heroic peal again,
Lo! useful industries now reign;—
Hark! labors mighty anthem strain
Rolls loud and long, nor rolls in vain,—
Sweeter than voices of the air,
That Loves' soft notes delicious bear!
Vast mingling energies combined,
Great forces, fire, earth, water, wind,
In unison with thundering sound,
Stir, thrill the riven globe around;
Telling of grand achievements won,—
Of Triumphs, Glory, just begun!
While mightiest forces mark man's way,
Great actor, in Life's drama-play;
Transcendant maxims wise and good,
Conserve high intellectual food;
Man's deeper consciousness supreme,
Touched by Truth's pure, eternal beam,
Bright, flaming essences of thought
To nobler Illiud's are wrought;

Grand images, similitudes,
Enchantment's grace, rapture's sweet moods,
Beauty's fair forms,—the soft, sweet glow,
Of arching iris, emerald bow,
Heaven's lovely, lordly, regal dyes,
Imaginations ecstacies,
Philosophy, high-browed and strong,
Pouring rich nectar-streams along;
These now supplant the buskings old,
The times demanding diamond, gold,
Perfection's charms, that garland life,
On laurels resting, freed from strife!
Already wrung from hopes forlorn,
Time's grander era here is born,
Knocks at each door, with earthquake sound,
Startles the nations far around!
Hark! 'tis the tramp of living men,
Quaffing Life's crystal tides again,—
In ranks of millions, brave and free,
Their footsteps west for Liberty!
Great lightnings falling from the sky,
Upheavings, clashings, day-springs nigh,
Deep, deepening thunder-peals rolled by,
Than ground to dust choosing to die,

Pass to the flaming worlds on high,
To victory's banquet in the sky,—
Win Glory's cloudless starry prize,
In splendor,—Glory,—endless rise!—
Like great Avatar, in his pride,
His garments red in vengeance dyed,
Long plunged 'neath mountain weight of woe,
For ages in his progress slow;
Lo! now he grasps his flashing blade,
In starry conqueror's robes arrayed,—
His fiery charger, glittering steed,
Rides on the storm, with lightning speed;
With flashing crest, ensigns unfurled,
Darts o'er the deep, the western world;
With fiat strong rolls back the tide
Of desolation, long defied,
On meteor beam, flames through the sky,
To victor tasks that never die,
Bursts Heaven's bright starry gates amain,
Deliverer scours th' eternal plain!
They come from wormwood, blood, and gall,
Draughts drunk in dismal tyrant thrall,
The palsying death-sigh, groan and fear,
Extinguished Hope, fell black despair,

From century-wrongs of toil and care,
Roused by the shout of mighty host,
Brave, valiant nations' Freedom's boast,
Their watchword, onset, patriot cry
Eternal Right, God, Liberty !
Tyrants wrenching from man victory,
'Mid other lands in distant climes,
Where destiny with age sublimes;
Vast empires reeling in the sun,
Advancement, progress, unbegun ;
A wilderness, a deadly sight
Of glittering spears, keen lances bright,—
Arms lifted still 'gainst fellow-man,
A bristling wall the centuries van ;
Ambition, jealousies, deep wrong,
Unbridled passions rampant, strong,
Still moving millions dark, inspire
To brandish ruin's torch of fire,—
Hurl missiles of devouring wrath,
And blot the sun from human path !
They come, they come, break seals of Time,
Inspired by hero acts sublime,
From every land, from every clime,
From Lybian wastes, from deserts vast,

From Norembega's stormy blast,
From ice-bound cliffs, from tropic shores,
From orient realms, with gems and ores,
From Indias, where dark Ganges pours,
From Chinee land, from far Cathay,
Where break the earliest beams of day;
From wiles that lie beneath the sun,
From poles where day scarce e'er begun,
From hillsides, plains, from mountains steep,
From lands along each hoary deep,
Where hurricanes, tornadoes sweep,
Isles, islets, gemming every sea,
A motley group for Liberty,—
Of varying accent, mother tongue,
The aged, infirm, the strong, the young,—
Complexion, shade of every dye,
Dark, flaxen-haired, black Saxon eye,
Fate, fortune, destinies, to try;
In thickening ranks, expectant throng,
Born by vast hero pride along,
Maxims, ideas, fatherland,
Gross, rude, imperial, convulsed, grand
Philosophies, art, literatures,
Unhomogenial mental lures,

With idiosyncrasies of mind,
Diverse as physical combined,
All crossed by living lines of fire,
Through ancestor, through son from sire,
Inlaid with Life's mysterious gold,
Great hero nuggets mined from old,
Ebullient energies, whence trace
A composite t' excel the race !
Drops now the past its mighty shield,
Time opes a new, more fertile field,
Selecter aims, motives inspire,
Kindles a new Promethean fire,
Dawns a blest age, of Love and zeal,
Grander still grows the common weal,—
Gigantic power begins new stride,
For vast dominion, empire wide,
Beyond the ancient chivalry,
In realms for man, enfranchised, free !
New work is given to human care,
Blind superstitions powerless are,
Apollo can no more divine,—
No Pythian dame from tripod whine,
Great Babylonish Gods of yore
Are worshiped, reverenced no more ;

Proud deities of Greece, of Rome,
Are shelterless without a home,
Minerva proud, with warrior crest,
Pan, who the sylvan shades once blest;
E'en Jupiter, of sovereign nod,
No more can falsely play the God!
Time tears away each sham, disguise,
Truth, reason, conquer pagan lies.
An age steals on superbly grand,
With Glory's brightening lusters spanned;
Mankind instructed from above,
Deep-moved by Faith, sweet hope and Love,—
To nobler acts and labors tend,
Their powers in useful service spend!
No astrologic giddy themes,
Of conjuring magic's fancy dreams;
Man's sobered reason's fire consumes;
No alchemyst's bewildering fumes
Of subtle essence, Time illumes,
Dark, ghostly nonsense now unplumes
For sober fact, tremendous Law,
Things scoffing doctors never saw
Or dreamed, in all their rambling mood,
To find the True,—the Fair,—the Good.

'Twas left for rarer, keener eyes,
Of penetration deep and wise,
Ages to light, instruct, surprise,
Give lessons of true, deep'ning lore,
Of knowledge bright'ning evermore,
Knowledge that sparkles, gems with light,
Priceless, moving the worlds aright!
Franklin disarms the bolted sky,
Brings down the electric courser shy,
Makes nervous women shake and cry,
With dreadness, terror wildly sigh,
His pandemonium bringing nigh,
The lightning flames, zigzag to try;
While Morse and Field now bid them fly,
Flash lightning Truth to every eye,
To hemispheres where e'er they lie,
'Neath ocean depths, o'er mountains dry,
Great flag of Washington on high,
The waving folds without a stain,
In triumph borne o'er land and main:
Sweet cynosure, cent'ring Earth's gaze,
Winning exultant homage, praise!
From riven chains the bondmen rise
With lifted hands, with streaming eyes,

Fling to the winds distrustful hate,
With generous knowledge crown their state;
Joyous from forced submission start,
Dare manlike deeds with patriot heart,
Shout to the centuries Freedom's song,
Roll Time's great jubilee along!
Sweet, blest humanities fast grow
On dark Oppression's overthrow,
New cords of love, deep, strong, entwine,
New, sweet amenities bright shine;
The charms of life fast multiply,
As wrongs, as ignominies die:
A fragrance falls from every breeze,
As man, his brother equal sees,
Blest with his birth-right, with a name
Nobler than Kings' on scrolls of fame!
Heard is Heaven's voice, felt power supreme,
Truth's radiant banners wave and stream,
Bright flashing symbols sparkle, gleam,
Borne on the air, through vaulted sky,
They draw the hoping myriads' eye;
In each desponding, downcast heart,
Bid Hope, new-fledged, assurance start,
Heal each bruised spirits sickening woe,   .

With Life's new nectar-draughts' o'erflow.
Eternal Right, Heaven's touchstone power,
Impregnates, moulds, shapes, guides the hour,—
Rare splendors fall, Truth's budding rod,
Bright, lustering, speaks the will of God;
Time's day of triumph near at hand,
When mightiest monuments o'erspanned
With deep'ning light, divinely planned,
Bright-beaconed by this western land,
Shall from foundations massive rise,
The nations charm, take by surprise.
That triumph's dawning beams e'en now
Fall on the sleepers' marble brow,
Waking from drowsy slumbers long
To hear the doom, the crash of Wrong,
The falling dynasties of woe,
Of tyrannies in overthrow!
The sleep of ages breaks at last,
Lo! mighty omens thicken fast,
Omens, bright wonders, erst unknown,
Through Time,—with prodigies thick strown,
Omens to blessing, peace, allied
To culture, growth, good, far and wide;
Omens of love, of Light divine,

That in celestial beauty shine,
Bright-flaming, radiant, matchless, all,
Zoning in brightness Time's dark ball;—
Omens of power, just, true and wise,
Bidding the nations wake and rise,
Burst ancient thraldoms, hail each ray
Prophetic of that coming day,
When truth shall reign with power supreme,
Earth be re-lit by Heaven's own beam !
Thick flash the rays from that bright sun,
An age of Glory here begun,
Far flaming, in its morning hour,
Bright with advent of new-born power,—
A power through ages past unknown,
Here in a day collossal grown,
Starting to run career more grand
Than e'er was dreamed in ancient land ;—
Accomplishing Heaven's will sublime,
O'erturning, purging guilt and crime,
Giving new prospects to mankind,
The dawn of centuries, great, refined !
Here freedom's battlements raised high,
A world in arms could mock, defy,
Hurl kingdoms, dynasties in dust,

In dreadest terror on them burst,
Sink in oblivious, endless shame,
They who dare man to curse, defame!
Here Peace with gentle olive wand,
White-starred, white-plumed, safe guards the
      land,
Science, invention, swift in turn,
Grand, glorious incense brightening burn,
Great powers, grand elements combined
In arts alembic, purged, refined,—
Give to man's arm Herculean force,
Make conqueror,—quicken Time's course;—
Discovery, with stalwart brow,
Scouts tropic heat, dares polar snow,—
Earth, air, the sky, the boundless sea,
Yield up their contents to the free;
Knowledge, Heaven-born, with radiant shrine,
Unfolds deep mysteries, themes divine,
With beams full-orbed, its splendors shine,
New, brighter garland-wreaths entwine,
Vast piercing tones, in thunder break,
The tottering dynasties now shake,
Caught by surprise, stunned, in amaze,
Thought sets the earth re-crowned ablaze!

Genius sublime erects new throne,
Pours deepening harmonies unknown,
Speaks with new voice,—Time's sovereign
        Power
Lights flaming beacons on its tower,
Insnared by no false flattering lures,
The general culture, good, insures:
Mysterious energy! supreme!
A splendor fired with Heaven's own beam,
Inlaid with radiant, beauteous Life,
Grand power that moulds the epoch's strife,
That guides the centuries' deepening stream,
That gives Time's waters sparkle, gleam;
Builder of periods, cycles grand,
The pride, the glory of each land!
It new creates this lower world,
Empires evokes, dashed, dismal, whirled
From ruin's vortex, high to rise,
Effulgent shine, chastised, made wise!
Mines Truth original, vast, deep,
Themes spousal, progenied, to sweep
Through unborn centuries of Time,
Germing great harvest hopes sublime!
Nations afar by passion tossed,

Seeking redress, their weapon's crossed;
As comes Time's swelling, patriot band,
Asylum make this western land;
Rushing from all the lands afar,
Lead by proud Freedom's blazing star,
It here degrades barbaric steel,—
Bids all for union fire their zeal,—
Seek amities, true friendship, peace,—
Feuds, plots, ambitions dark, surcease;
To trace on every banner bright,
That holiest word, Eternal Right,
For that when called, march in the van,
Nor e'er desert the cause of man;
Tells to the world's great list'ning ear,
In accents heard through every sphere,
That bright'ning shafts of deathless Fame
With holier light gild Worth's proud name;
That threadbare Custom finds no place,
Sinks by its weight, its own disgrace,
Each luckless usage starred with ill,
In vain past sphere attempts to fill;
Contrivances from Ignorance' loom,
Meet with misfortune's common doom;
Bald Prejudice with sun-bleared eye,

Old moss-grown forms, grown sere and dry,
Dread edicts of tyrannic power,
Fly from before Time's bright'ning hour!
Creeds of outgrown, unmeasured length,
Wax feeble, lose their waning strength;
Concocted mischiefs, world-wide grown,
Their noxious germs through ages strown,
Barked,—with their vain, their vast conceit,
Now doomed, find overthrow complete!
Dark day of Bigotry is past,
Faith, Reason, Common Sense, at last,
Wisdom, escaped from Folly's stool,
O'er Error, Superstition, rule!
Firm, just, unchanging, flexile too,
The Pilgrim Sires, they seek the true,—
They trace Heaven's vast, infinite thought,
Its treasures rare, ages have wrought,
Ages all dark, that prized them not,
With prejudice, with folly fraught,
That blindly dim, and mar and blot!
The Pilgrims sound the sparkling mine,—
Investigation,—plummet,—line,—
With mind absorded, in hungering mood,
Stirred with deep sense for spiritual food,

Truth's finer forms elect, perceive,
By faith embrace, digest, believe,
Drink from pure fountains born on high,
That slake when human waters dry;
'Mid overarching, pearly light,
Trace Time's great future opening bright,
Drop influence, whose onward flow
Shall wide expand, through centuries go,
Pregnant with graces, rich and sweet,
Yet crown a world at Jesus' feet!
Say not, O Godless, doubting age,
When selfish passions, lust, and rage,
When love, obedience, faith, pure zeal,
For righteousness, the common weal,
To sinister ends must yield away,
Devoutness to some trifle, play,
To legerdemain, the cunning hand,
Fantastic tricks, deceptions bland,
Rank prurience, with glut'nous greed,
Strewing broadcast all poisonous seed,
For harvests, centuries to feed,
On nonsense, fooleries' sickening weed,
When age, once honored, grand, sublime,
Dissocialized, is made a crime,—

The hoary head of Righteousness
Heaven owns, delights e'ermore to bless,
Crowns, blossoming in virtue,—Truth,
Despised by beardless, silly youth,
Cursed, lampoon'd, without conscience, shame,
By villainies without a name!
While all should hail, with fond acclaim,—
Alas, alas! who is to blame?
Has not authority grown tame?
Unlike the time when Pilgrims came,
Parental government is lame,
Unlit by Glory's dazzling flame,
Heaven's benizon,—eternal shame,
An age with scandal to defame!
O, say not fathers were severe,
While ruin's surge is rolling near;
When sons to fathers law declare,
And zigzag sapplings;—O, beware
Of rocky reefs, of quicksand shore,
Of breakers wrecking evermore!
The Pilgrim Genius, grand and strong,
Builds for the ages, centuries long,
For grand developments unseen,
When earth shall flood with Glory's sheen,

When Time, when Nature, robed in light,
Shall register great annals bright,
Strong pledge of that supernal day
When veils from sense shall fall away,
Immortal consummations found
Of human hopes, on hallowed ground!

They saw vast, inward harmonies of life,
Beyond all outward jarrings, noise and strife,
Treading the verge of that supernal sphere,
To thought, to spirit dear,—
In rapt, transcending mood they rise and soar,
Gaze on vast breaking splendors, rolling bright,
Pure realms of unborn day,—
Dateless, without decay,—
Where stainless, purged, the radiant throngs
    adore,
In shining groups, flashing immortal beams,
Heaven's axle 'neath their fiery teams,
Eager, all panting for empyrean flight!
There, 'mid the vast, the infinite, serene,
Where high accords, deep cadences loud roll,
Nought spirit, mind, the pastime, joy, between,
All one vast carnival of soul,

Whose rising tides of bliss they feel,
Waking with inward passion, zeal;
There, as they gaze, catch visions of the blest,
Incorporate, pass, taste the celestial rest,
Transform, transfigure, upward rise,
Deep soul-thirst finding full supplies,
Opening all spirit, eye, to Light,—
Ends beings' awful night,—
They feel new, quickening power, a love sub-
    lime,
Whose deep'ning flames wake, warm and thrill,
Nerving for conflicts 'gainst all ills of Time,
New symmetries of Life enweave, enclothe, and
    fill,
Make champions,—grander than Time e'er
    bore.
Scan we the ages o'er,—
Bright'ning as Heaven's purpose, power and
    strength instill!
Full-fledged, gigantic, drinking living Force,
O'er thrones, false dynasties, they take their
    course,
Touched by supernal beams of endless day,
They fling the scaffoldings of power away;

All elemental goodness, wide, around,
Transfuse, inmix, ingrain, deep inly blend,
With piercing brightness stir the fallow ground,
From crystal springs streams send,—
Vast boundaries prepare
To wave with harvest-home for all mankind,—
Fair fruits, chaste excellencies, well refined,
Time's golden bounties rare!
The Grand, Select, the Good,
Man's high immortal food
Alone can satisfy,—
They, the grand boon acquiring,—
Long ages dark inspiring,—
With Light, with Life, Time's mightiest heralds
    strong,
They wake terrene, celestial song,—
Through trial's stormy night
They shine, grow in immortal radiance, bright!

In converse with ideal realms sublime,
Small, grand magnificences of all time,
Hearing the voice of Heaven's all-waking
    truth,
Bright with perennial youth,—
  4

All else they scorn, as baseness, frothing foam,
Shorn of great elements, vitalities that warm,
Wanting celestial fire,—
Power man to move, inspire,—
Dark bitter-sweet, no royal honey-comb,
Base, fragile mockeries of sapless Earth,
Death-struck, at moment of their birth,
The ghostly phantoms that through centuries
    swarm;
Higher than Time's chill, ever-blighted ground,
Beyond the visible, dark curtained sky,
Passing celestial hemispheres around,
Bursting with forms that never die,—
On rapt, seraphic, tireless wing,
Ideal treasures vast they bring,—
Plant deepest solitudes of hoary Time,
Germs soon to burst, proud trellis climb,
Unfold in grand creations bright,
Enchantment to each gazer's sight;
Enweave fair bowers of magic pride,
To Heavenly forms allied;—
Flaming with quenchless zeal, with passion
    fired,
Moved by sweet power, selectest virtues tried,

For superhuman labors Heaven-inspired,
All wrathful elements of nature, man, defied,
Through them in wonder nations gaze, behold
Deeds grander than of old,—
Bright, sparkling streams of Good, poured
    through creation wide !
Lifting the race from its low groveling seat,
Time's mighty work perfecting, incomplete,
Sublimed with harmonies, they sweet control,
With rapture's fires wake each benighted soul;
Down-steering from seraphic heights above,
When courage halts, when power frowns dis-
    may,
Through potent energies of mighty Love,
They cut their garland way,—
Fearless of all they see,—
Seizing Truth's scepter, brightening rod,
Instinct with essence of a present God,
They conquer, and are free !
Their's Time's grand royal prize,
Name, Fame, that never dies ;
Heroic triumphs grand,—
Their work all unassuming,—
Centuries through them fresh blooming,—

No coming period, epoch, but shall tell
The charm of their victorious spell:
How through the seas of old
They came, and brought Time's crowning age
    of gold!

Deep, inmost avenues of power supreme,
They tread 'neath Light's supernal flashing
    beam,
With martyr-spirit hold high upward way,
Pilgrims to endless day;—
Yielding all forms to spirit, quickening life,
They dare vast bounds, by mortals all untrod,
Fan to rapt flame desire,—
With beatific fire,—
Commune, hold converse, 'mid dark elemental
    strife,
With starry ministries of Light, Heaven's
    host,
In mighty quest, 'mid deepening splendors
    lost,—
Through dreadest storms, behold a smiling
    God!
Casting firm hold within the clefted Rock,

While dash and foam dark waves of billowy
    Time,
Nathless though ills, dark destinies, may
    mock,—
They waft on crystal seas sublime,—
Finding sweet gales, Elysian air,
Bright scenes immortal, blooming fair,
While 'round terrific whirlwinds madly blow
The seething foam, they perils never know;
Shielded by Heaven's eternal power,
In vain the angry tempests lower,
Like Israel, th' engulphing sea
Ne'er harms God's chosen free!
Great seers, great sages, to their conscience true,
Feeling incoming strength, nerving each soul,
Their hands wax strong, tempestuous passage
    through,
Exultant while dark crashing waters round
    them roll!
Ordained by Heaven to set new seals to Fate,
Onward they steer elate,
'Till their frail bark drops anchor by the
    wished for goal!
Enrapt, entranced, by melodies divine,

Charmed by great falling lusters bright that
  shine,
Roused, thrilled, by Time's far-loudening thun-
  der peal,
Their great commission stamped with Heav-
  en's high seal,
They plan in hollow'd Jehovah's hand;
The furious elements that line their path
Urge onward to the Heaven-sought, promised
  land,
Preserve from tyrant wrath,
'Till thronging ignominies great,
O'er past, in fellowship with righteous power,
A hemisphere they plant, a world endower,
Build Time's true-founded State!
Ineffable their toil,
They proud, fierce tyrants spoil,—
Open earth's hero path,—
Time's mightiest wrongs undoing,—
Great common weal pursuing,—
Lift they proud Freedom's standards high, un-
  furled,
To future ages point a world,
While man, nations revere

The founders of the Western Hemisphere!

Through their high wisdom, healthful rule,
Exemplars bright of modern school,
Lo! Time's great epoch is begun;
Wakes the vast world 'neath Freedom's sun,
Sublimer race man starts to run,
To reach the goal that shall be won!
See mightiest forces meet and play,
Where else were pomp, wild, mock display.
Great fire-horse thunders through the land,
Trailing its steam-cloud banner grand,
Ploughs the vast ocean's molten plain,
Whose storms and billows rage in vain;
Along the vital, thymy air,
Electric forces tidings bear,
Th' unsunned, unstarred, mysterious deep,
Where sea-gods secret conclaves keep,
Its ancient silence yields profound
The lightning thought darting earth round!
Winds, waves and air, the sunlight sweet,
Are flung, proud trophies, at man's feet,
The elements, long warring, bow,
Nature's grand forces wreathe his brow!

With powers supernal, vast, refined,
A thinking, an immortal mind,—
All mightiest energies he plies,
All systems, methods, fearless tries,
Waits on the tempest, as it flies,
Pierces eclipses with keen eyes,
Gives Fortune myriad-changing dyes,
Wins by routine, by grand surprise,
Ne'er lost for themes, plans to devise,
That he aggrandized, high may rise,—
Born for great deeds, starred victories,
Sublimest, grandest destinies!
Man mounts on pinions, proud to fly,
He soars to bright'ning worlds on high,
Mysteries exhausts, of earth and sky,—
Through the vast, noiseless realms of space
Renews the fabled giants' race,
Traces the flaming worlds that roll,
Suns, stars, vast orbs to either pole,
Surveys infinitudes of Light,
Bursting with constellations bright,
Courts mystic veil that shrouds God's throne,
All Heaven's bright sapphire, purple zone,
The star-dropt curtains unuplift,

Whither his higher passions drift;—
Creation's boundaries travels o'er,
Gazing on wonders evermore,
Infinite footprints, everywhere
Prompting Devotion's grateful prayer.
Wearied, with labors, cares oppressed,
His dire transgressions, sins, confessed,
He knocks at Heaven's unbarred gate,
Where Mercy's squadroned angels wait,
Enters, re-born, seals there his trust,
A spirit clothed in mortal dust;
Leans his proud head on Love's bright form,
Nor fears doom's threat'ning, vengeful storm!
Nor does his silence then begin,
When burst the bands of hateful sin;
Amid his bliss he cease to know,
In knowledge endless, born to grow.
Lo! then he waxes grave and wise,
In themes deep-quarried 'mid the skies,
In spiritual doctrines, mysteries, taught,
In theologic battle caught,
He nerves with firmness 'gainst distraught;
With pointed shaft, with foremost thought,
Prepares for bloodless, bold onslaught;

Against blasphemer's Godless lore,
Barking, like Cerberus, at Hell's door,
Lo! now he argues, holds debate,
On mutable, predestinate,
On sovereign will, God's purpose great,
On Freedom, blind decrees of Fate,
With reason, argument, conspires
To light Truth's waning altar fires,—
Cultured in logic, sharp, profound,
Hurls ranting skeptics to the ground;
With metaphysic scissors bright
He champions eternal Right,
Unravels sophistries and fraud,
Pointing, " Thus saith the Word of God,"
That Word that breaks with Heavenly light,
Dissolving, flooding Earth's midnight,
Whose bright, transforming, quenchless beam,
Blushing with supernatural gleam,
In haloing splendor e'er to stream,
In radiance bright till kingdoms fall,
Satanic o'er Earth's blackened ball!
Thus is an age august advanced,
All humbler periods out-distanced;
Wit, sarcasm, satire, withering, bold,

By master skill quick'ning a world,
While vulgar arts cease not to thrive,
Swarming e'ermore the human hive!
Does contemplation joy at sight
Of new-born scenes, transcending bright,
Each pensive, sad, dejected heart
Thrill, feel new pulse-tides throb and start?
Turned from all sick'ning sights away,
Let all behold Time's grand display,—
Its mighty forces, agents, power,
Re-'lume, and bless the deep'ning hour,
See wondrous strides of genius, skill,
Their great'ning destinies fulfil,
The high achievements, wrought by care,—
Grace, Beauty, Honor, virtues rare,
The crowning fruit, select, they bear!
The cultured fields, their waving plume,
The roseate garden's spiced perfume,
The crown of ages, barbarous, wild,
Here worn by Freedom's giant child!
Nor has the world outleaped its place,
In meteor flight forgot the race,
Dissolved the kindred ties that bind
In unity of life, mankind;—

Not, not alone do ages stand,
They grow in league, alliance grand,
Have kindred sympathies, one aim,
One in true glory, virtuous fame,
One life,—one lot,—Truth to proclaim,—
One work, to vindicate its claim.
Amid this onward sweep of power,
Voices that thrilled Time's earlier hour
In tones of pathos, grandeur sweet,
Th' advancing periods proudly greet!
Unroll proud History's pictured page,
Th' Athenian, Roman's grandest age,
There germs of matchless power unfold,
There Freedom stirred the fires of old,
There blushed in dawn an age of gold!
Lo! voices grand like ocean's swell,
Thunder, entrance, with magic spell,
Instruct, teach lessons to the race,—
Proud feats of valor, beauty, grace,
Tell how grand Eloquence, sublime,
Burst forth, appalling monarchs' crime,—
How Poesy, forever young,
Its clarion blast creative rung,
Through Homer, God-like Illiads sung,

Kindled imagination's fire,
Lighted a torch ne'er to expire,—
From dread Achilles' wrathful ire,—
Sent forth a flame through earth to run,
Hailed by all lands beneath the sun!
How Art beheld triumphal day,
When Phidias flung immortal ray,
Time's temple decked with garlands sweet,
Which passing centuries hail and greet;—
How Plato, with a soul of fire,
The honey-lipped, whom gods inspire,
Dropping sweet, flashing pearls of Truth,
Gave History's page immortal youth,
Ideal thoughts, in beauty dressed,
So chaste, with grace, sweetly expressed,
Elysian speech whose magic spell
Stirs inmost harmonies of soul,
'Till diapasons whispering roll
Melodious chimes through balmy air,
And mind transfigures flowering fair!
How, 'mid vast pillars, column'd aisles,
The Bema wreathed with patriot smiles,
Parthenon famed through lands and isles,
Loud Demosthenic thunders pealed,

And mightiest senates shook and reeled!
Great, mighty voices of the Past,
Of deepening accent unsurpassed,—
Melodious, musical, they thrill,
Warn, teach, instruct, enlighten still!
They sound heroic deeds of yore;
When heard we live the ages o'er;—
Tell how great Brutus held proud sway,
Great Cæsar killed one awful day,
Filling dread tyrants with dismay,
As empire shot rekindling ray,
And Rome imperial bounds away,
With new-born destinies in play!
How Cicero with patriot fire,
Blasts Cataline's malignant ire,
While deathless Virgil, Mantuan bard,
His country warms, with chaste regard,—
How Horace, Ovid, charmed, beguiled,
And Terence, as the muses smiled,
How Coriolanus, from the field,
Through prowess, valor, empire sealed,—
How Regulus, how Scipio great,
Bound dazzling garlands round the State;
And later, 'mid the wrecks of Time,

Daring great patriot deeds sublime,
How, crowned by living martyr fame,
Rienzi won immortal name,
Where art, immortal, smiles in bloom,
Survives, and decks an empire's tomb!
Great voices resonant with power,
They thrill, enrich Time's onward hour,
Fall on the lands with witchering spell,
Listening as peals their magic swell,
To learn the mighty tale they tell ;
What crashing forces, vast, sublime,
Have swept along these realms of Time,—
What dynasties of guilt expire,
'Neath public vengeance' roused ire,
What empires vanish, pass away,
Through dark injustice, godless sway,
What kingdoms come, rejuvenesce,
Dart living beams mankind to bless,—
What usage, custom, order grand,
Shall yet illume each unblessed land,—
Earth with new light to be o'er-spanned!
The deathless beams of human lore,
They flash from lands that genius bore,
Transfiguring mounts of Glory, Fame,

Starred with immortal, heroes name,—
The Past's great struggle trace, review,
Great crowning conquests ope anew,
Tell what convulsions dire have sprung,
How mightiest changes have been wrung,
Time's mighty acts in epics sung,
Immortal, deathless, ever young !
Ages they vast experience span,
Fling hope-lights to o'er-burdened man,
Quicken his vast, advancing tread,
The mighty voices of the dead !
Those voices break, we hear their peal,
The fires of ages through us steal,—
Tell of vast labors proudly done,
Of victories, triumphs, grandly won;
Their deathless echoes deepening swell,
In diapason thunder, tell
To unborn ages Time's great deed,
Man, from dread bondage, tyrants feed !
Voices of deep, grand, swelling power,
Pour'd from dim realms, creation o'er,
With deepening repercussing sound,
Passing great hemispheres around;
They waken homage, vast, profound,

From centuries, their blazing mound,
Distil rare sweets on modern ground,
They give the world, mankind new bound,
To Life's grand music richer sound,
Whose cords all swept sweetly resound,
As oneness, unity are found !
Man, human nature, grow refined,
Through deep affinities combined,
The great cognations deeply lie
In depths unscanned by mortal eye;
Great golden veins, deep-starring shine,
Th' abyss of Being make divine;
Cords of vibration in the soul,
Humanity proclaim a whole;—
There are great undertones of life,
Heard in the calms of mortal strife;
Sounding in each bright spirit's ear,
They hush forebodings, terrors, fear,
Send their electric, magic thrill,
With life each power, each passion, fill !
The lily warmed by sun-lit air,
Blushes with heavenliest graces rare;
Bright diamond quarried from the mine,
Blest with day-beams, will sparkle, shine:

5

Mind bright, more radiant, beaming, fair,
Than earth-born charms, distinctions are,
Blest by a quickening beam, fond strain,
Fair blushes, binds sweet golden chain
Of sympathy, of union bright,
Grows beauteous 'neath falling light
Of ages, whose loud voice afar
Is sweet, as is a rising star!
Rare qualities, bright charms of life,
Flower from the centuries' bloody strife,
Through kindred perils, glories, passed,
Enweave the touchstone graces last!
Sweet undulating hills arise,
Great mountain grandeurs pierce the skies;
The leaf, the bud, then golden corn,—
Earth first from tempest, chaos, born;
Then iris, rainbow, sweet adorn,—
Time in its matchless, massive tread,
Weaves brightening garlands round its head;
Advances e'er man's powerful race
Stable the good, great wrongs efface,
The offal, chaff, vile refuse burns,
Each lustering gem more lust'rous turns!
Let wisdom, knowledge, virtue grow,

The world puts off its weeds of woe;
Blossom rare judgments, maxims wise,
Dark error, doomed, sickens and dies:—
Mingling rare elements divine,—
In new-born splendor nations shine,
Grand royal charms renew, refine,
Fair, fair the laurels they entwine;
Genius, its radiant sparkling mine,
Blazing along the centuries' line;
The mighty ages of the Past,
They meet, they triumph here at last!
'Tis with the braided cords of Time
We bind our brow with wreaths sublime,
The beauteous Fair, the lovely, grand,
By Heaven's Great Architect deep planned,
Enrich all mental, moral food,
Deepen true culture, spiritual mood,
Man's hungering thirst for endless good,
E'er since Time's pillars heaved have stood,—
Nor till God's universe shall change,
Shall His deep plans e'er disarrange.
What true has been from error freed,
To Progress joined, solves human need,
The mighty problems of mankind,

By Past, by Present, are defined,—
Great triumphs, sorrows, joys passed o'er,
But limn great ages just before,
Each Heaven-born impulse of man's soul
In closest ties e'er binds the whole,—
Speaks to all ranks, howe'er arrayed,
Of kindred blood and being made!

The Pilgrims—they were of the immortal few
Ordained by Heaven the ages to renew,—
Delving in specious ores, while nations stood,
They seek the True and Good,—
Round Time's horizon, glance with piercing
　　gaze,
With trustful spirit, a subdueless aim,
Seize the ripe hour of Fate,—
Heroic, grandly great,
Flashing Truth's bright, creative rays,
They tread the cheerless paths of dimming
　　Time,—
Great Past, great Present, join in choral chime,
Though long despised, sure of mankind's ac-
　　claim!
Bold sentinels on watch-towers moss-o'ergrown,

They catch sweet glimpses, as from mountain
    height,
Of rolling splendors in the vales unknown,
And from the Past, its visions bright,
See the great Future's emerald dawn,
Its peerless, radiant, purple morn;—
On Wisdom's burning mount, in its great name,
They light their kindling torch, bear on the
    flame,
Through gorge, through chasm, opening wide,
Re-light the altars that had died,
With Truth's eternal, changeless beam,
Giving it power supreme!
Great, Heaven-born seers, to guide man's on-
    ward way,—
High Priests of deep'ning intellectual light,—
Watching for full-orbed splendors of the day,
Sublimely musing o'er dissolving realms of
    night,
They stamp the waves of darkness 'neath their
    feet,
The coming centuries greet,—
Unseal their breaking glories, quenchless ra-
    diance bright!

Grand themes they urge, born to enrich the
　　race,——
With heavenly zeal Time's mightiest problems
　　trace,——
Vast, deep, profound, mysterious, grand, sub-
　　lime,——
Throning th' eternal 'bove these sparks of
　　Time.
Through them the changeless tide of Progress
　　moves
With high benevolence to every land,
Through free-born acts, not rigid iron grooves,
Showing God's mighty hand ;——
They from the centuries call,
With Beauty's spotless robes nations enshroud,
Cover with Glory's unconsuming cloud,——
While earth's dark fetters fall !
Their's Time's triumphal way,
Pompless, without display,
'Neath Heaven's cerulean arch,——
Rousing all lands their bearing,——
Time's mightiest good declaring,——
Resistless, onward, is the power they gave,
While empires toss, and fall the brave,

They never dim nor die,
Their names enrolled, entablatured on high!

Vast, new-born Power, colossal in their might,
Endless in resource to maintain the Right,
Stainless, unbribed, unfettered, virtuous, strong,
Wiping away Time's wrong,—
Peerless they lift new broadside to the world,
Marshal new virtues, check ambition's lust,
Beyond dark dimming lines,
Rude ignorance defines,
With Heaven's bright symbols high unfurled,
Distrustful of the Past, its blind control,
They designate man's grander goal,
Round which Time's deep'ning splendors burst!
On new foundations build the Social Life,
The general good subordinating all,
The world around with dire contentions rife,
Seeking all lands to disenthral,
To mightiest germs planted 'mid night,
Truth's radiant, dropping lusters bright,
They turn, from Heaven's vast store-house
      draw
Whate'er conserves high order, virtuous law;—

'Mid Nature's temple, through its door,
With beaming foreheads bowed t' adore,
High acts of adoration steal,
Secure the common weal:—
A mighty host, in numbers faintly small,
All that is glorious, grand, they well combine,
Trace on grand scale for kingdoms, countries,
    all,
'Round great'ning destinies proud garland
    wreaths entwine,—
Nor through devotion cease their mighty task,
Panting in light to bask,
Till born vast blessings that the race upbuild,
    refine!
With growing warmth they sound the unre-
    vealed,
Break Time's vast secret fate, by them unsealed,
Pour light on darkness, cheer the glorious
    brave,
Roll on great Freedom's sparkling, flashing
    wave!
Their power pure, noiseless, as the balmy
    light,
Grand as the ocean in its mighty swell,

Sun-like, tracing fair myriad blossoms bright,
On mountain, hill, in dell,—
Great champions of the free,
They break the iron yokes Oppression bound,
Far, far, the vast, the wide creation round,
Give nations liberty!
Ne'er 'neath grand Roman arch
Did conquering heroes march,
Such wonder, joy, inspire,—
They the great Past repairing,
From tyrants' scepters tearing,—
Their course, 'twas as a new-born beam of
    light,
Piercing pollution's starless night,
Waking sweet, rapturous strain,
The virtues dead returned to life again!

Great Pilgrim band, they rise beyond compare
With times that have been, or that passing are;
Born for no age, but for mankind at large,
They bear Time's mightiest charge,
Nor seem amazed at greatness of their deed,
Supremely blest, though Fortune ne'er en-
    dower

With kingly diadem,
Or monarch's purple hem ;—
Their dower, vast, mighty nations freed,
The endless sympathies of Goodness born,
All that can dignify, adorn,—
A world enfranchised from dread tyrant
　　power!
Saw ye the Orient with its purple gleam,
Where breaks the eye of Day through roseate
　　light,
Where scarlet, amber clouds, God's banners,
　　stream,
The gilding pomp of morning bright ;—
Where sunbeams flame, the summits climb,
And pierce the morass, bogs, of Time,
Till from proscenium darkening veil
Uplift, vast splendors o'er creation sail,
Roll on in bright, majestic stride,
Light Nature's landscape far and wide,
Bright pledge of harvests evermore,
Bringing vast golden store !
Thus the great Pilgrim host, its work sublime
With life, with beauty, grandeur, welling o'er,—
Deliverers grand of blackened realms of Time,

They shed new mental, moral light, on king-
    doms pour,
Rise on a darkened world, with light re-born,
Renewing hopes forlorn,—
Kindling sweet hopes, where all was night and
    gloom before !
As some great organ in cathedral tower,
Discoursing music, grand assuaging power,
Touched by the master hand, pipe, timbrel,
    string,—
Soon all around respond, dome, arches ring,
They voice mankind, their accents grow su-
    preme,
Ruling by Wisdom's unobstructed sway ;
Sweet as grand organ's peal, with joy's bright
    gleam,
They scatter doubts away,—
Open new golden seat,
Where brighter glories break in grand amaze,
And pour sublime their gorgeous, pencilled
    rays,
Man's destinies complete !
Some grander sweep of Time
Must tell their fame sublime,

Great hero-martyr sires,—
With lofty aims conspiring,
Ages, mankind admiring,
Long, long as Glory's echoes loud shall steal,
And Time shall more and more reveal,
They of the chosen few
Shall e'er be found, to God,—man,—Duty, true!

E'en at the rising of their sun
Are new, sweet anthem-strains begun;
A new, bright age dawns on the world,
Truth, Glory's banners high unfurl'd,
Grander than when great Roman sire
Kindled with zeal at pagan fire;
Than when the mighty Grecian spoke,
Whose thrilling tones in thunder broke,—
Great age of Life, of moral Light,
Rolling vast splendors, pure and bright,
Sending afar to every land,
With science, art, God's great command,—
Giving to man, nations' new-birth,
Restoring Paradise to earth!
Hark! hear that mighty choral swell!
From every land where mortals dwell,—

Nations uprising in a day,
Casting their idol gods away,—
Dark Pagan tribes at Truth's great shrine,
Quaffing its living beams divine;
Mind, glorious mind, its fetters break,
With grand immortal themes awake;
Man treads a new, ascending sphere,
The great millenium draws near,— .
Knowledge, advancing, pours new light
O'er densest glooms of ancient night!
Great statesman now no longer plays
With Time's augmenting destinies,
Garlands his brow with virtue's ray,
Bids policies of fraud give way,
Seeks out an honored, bright'ning fame,
By breathing Truth's unspotted name!
The bard who wakes immortal lyre
No longer feeds base passion's fire,
Portrays grand themes of power sublime,
T' immortalize through coming time,
With culture, independence, flings
Defiance at the wrath of kings,
Toils, dedicates his deathless strain,
The slaves of bondage to unchain,

With sympathy his numbers flow,
Wake Heavenly joys 'mid realms of woe,—
Pour sweet frankincense Time along,
The path to Heaven fill with song;
Sway by the power of moral light,
Grow grandest in the cause of Right!
The great Historian stamps his page
With truths for an advancing age,—
No longer sickens human life
With worthless tales of savage strife;
Traces great central aims of power,
Forces that shape the onward hour,
Why revolutions spring profound,
Fling death, black ruin's arrows 'round,
Breaking with light of happier day,
Bearing the ancient wrongs away.
O'er the vast world with lambient flame,
Truth, Love, fast-flashing, star their name;
Kingdoms and crowns fast falling down,
Earth's tyrants flee, man gains renown;
An embryo spark of God's own fire,
His soul renewed with vast desire,
Dilates, still mightier good to bear,
Light the lone realms of dark despair,

Restore Heaven's long lost image there;
Take blood-stained shrines of guilt away,
'Mid darting beams, Heaven's dawning day,
While voices, thunders, earthquakes sound,
Love, Mercy triumph, earth around!
Whence, whence, this swelling, surging tide,
Borne through the lands, realms, far and wide,
Man, human nature's grandest pride,
Earth beaming joy from side to side?
Has some strange fantasy of light
Burst forth in meteor lusters bright?
Has some new conjuring minstrel spell
T' oblivion sent the shades to dwell?
Comes Time's great conqueror, in his might,
To consecrate grand age of Right,
Dart on mankind Truth's burning rays,
Fill future ages with its blaze?
No, 'twas th' immortal Pilgrim band
That lowly bowed on Plymouth's strand,—
They waved their ægis, heavenly bright,
And Time, the, ages fill with light!
In their immortal footsteps young,
Culture, Improvements, songs are sung,
Where, thro' the gloom, they broke their way,

Flames now the grandest orb of day,—
Great elemental centuries war,
Darkness primeval driven afar,—
Hills, vales, uplifted mountain land,
In deepening radiance, glory spanned,
New bud, new earing come apace,
Grand harvests ripening for the race.
No more shall man, nations, repine,
Selectest beams fast ray and shine,
Unseal new stores of moral good,
Warms intellect with nurturing food,—
New, vast creative realms of thought,
In kindling contact now are brought;
Along proud Nature's golden ways
Dart swift, electric, purging rays,
Sweet nectar-founts unseal and flow,
New raptures charm, comes end of woe;—
Sweet concords of ebullient life
Wax, still the storms of ancient strife
Tell that Perfection's goal afar,
Lights 'neath its radiant, glistening star,
That soon shall dawn its crowning day,
With grand effulgence earth shall sway.
Great hope-lights cheer, vast works abound,

Earth's center light, circumference round ;—
Works of surpassing grandeur, power,
Drop radiance on each passing hour,
Rare products of no envious brain,
Of tyrants, threatening still to reign :
Their day is past,—vile work is done,—
Sinks, fast retires their shading sun,
Their race accursed, 'tis quickly run,
Associate man now sovereign, chief,
He plans humanity's relief :—
The vile diplomacies are past,
New, conquering policies are cast
In Truth's eternal, changeless mould,
No human right in market sold!
Transcending principalities,
Kingdoms, their thrones, vast treasuries,
All, all the wealth that empires pile,
To which e'en globe itself is vile,
With all its hoard of shining gold,
Its wrapping splendors, fold on fold,
Its streaming purples, crimsons bright,
Its scarlet, emerald, amber white,
Its India, its Golconda gems,
Its Cæsar triumphs, diadems ;
6

Man, man alone waxes supreme,
For him bright, new-born symbols gleam,
For him new brightening banners stream.
Man,—grander than imperial state,
His worth, his value, ne'er t' abate,
Born to command, destined to rise,
Great lord of earth—his home the skies!
Who can the Pilgrim life declare,
Plumed as knight-errants never were,
Yet dashing ancient kingdoms through,
Establishing vast empire new.
No wild, impetuous, false crusade,
Armored in bristling steel they made,
Riding swift steeds, in gems, in gold,
Mettling with fire, fierce, daring, bold,
Fanatical to save a world,—
In Moslem vengeance caught and whirl'd,—
Performing feats of valor great,
Busying vain ages to relate :—
Their knightly armor was the Truth,—
In that they waked and slept from youth ;
Their arrows falling from the sky,
They bid them through creation fly ;
In dazzling radiance quenchless poured,

From the great shrine where they adored ;
Working as leaven, as light, like fire,
They nation's with vast thoughts inspire ;
Mankind they move, as shadows fall,
Changing their place upon the wall,—
With gentlest touch,—with influence grand,—
Time's dial pointing from their hand ;—
Loud as deep thunder, earthquake's knell,
Tyrants foredoom, their downfall tell,
Before upheavings, truthful power,
Despots they make to tremble, cower,—
Rid of monstrosities a world,
Baptized 'neath Freedom's flag unfurled !
Freedom, the savage tyrants' prey,
Driven from dawn of Time away
From human hearthstones, human lot,
Its royal pedigree forgot ;
Baptized in lineaments of wrath,
Made pander to oppression's path,
False minister to avarice, pride,
Ambition, plunder, stalking wide
O'er all the earth,—in grief, dismay,
The nations sick'ning with decay.
No gushing springs, no bounteous Life,

No verdure,—foul, dark passions rife;
No blissful impulse, quickening power,
Light streaming on Time's darkening hour;
Fierce, woful tempest, blackening storm,
Bowing to dust each mighty form!
Yet, through the guise of falsehood, shame,
Through centuries flashing dim its flame,
Its life unspent, an ocean deep,
Whose waters stirred cresting shall sweep
High o'er all crumbling wrecks of Time,
In grandeur, majesty sublime;
New blush of morn, tinging a world
With dyes of crimson, purple, gold,
They sanctify,—bid altars new,
Flash its bright beams the epochs through,—
With its invigorating air
The waste of ages long repair;
Build beacon-lights, high flaming tower,
'Long avenues of usurped power,
Darting its radiant heavenly beam,
Knowledge, blest Right, twin-born, supreme!
Society, foul, dismal, dark,
They warm with its unquenching spark,
With radiant virtues, charms encrown,

Plant its rare germs, enseal renown.
Freedom God's gift from Heaven above,
Great offspring of eternal Love,
On Time's hoar brow its garlands twine,
Through them the ages grow divine;
No misappliance, staining blot,
Huge malice, envies, fools have sought,
Infernal witchcrafts, horror's tale,
A momentary madness, gale,—
No blind proscription sending far
Some new, mayhap new rivalling star;
Justice with stern avenging lip,
The prudeless Quaker in its grip,
Suffice t' eclipse their growing fame,
Dim the sweet luster of their name.
The great, the wise, new force they gave
Expiring civilizations, save,—
The world's great hope, they build anew
By policies of wisdom true,
On generations fix their claim,
The selfish nations put to shame!
They swing a censor burning gold,
Create, make new, transform the old,
Ope channels for new light to shine,

Shape, mould the human by Divine,
Life's structures homogeneous raise,
Through sacrifice, faith, prayer and praise,
One beauteous temple yet to be
Proud home, great shrine of Liberty!
Each valued gift, beauty, delight,
They polish with celestial light;
All rules, relations that control,
Inbreathe with vitalizing soul
Of Truth's eternal spirit, fire;
They lift mankind, a world inspire
With thoughts transcendant, deeds that trace
The brightest path in glory's race!
Others had fought, and bled, and died,
The bloodiest tyrants foiled, defied,
Darted bright beams through nations far,
Been hailed mankind's bright morning star
Ascendant,—long to rise and reign,
Yet oft as seen, quick set again,—
The blush of morn cursed by swift doom,
Time one miscarriage from the womb,
Each smiling birth laid in the tomb
Ere its fair loveliness could bloom!
Pulsations grand, electric, stilled

Earth with returning darkness filled;—
While 'mid temptations, trial, night,
All schemes of hope, of promise, blight,
They stem the raging streams of Time,
And centuries their peans chime;—
They hold their course through night, till day
Drives all antagonisms away.
The barren soil, degenerate clod,
They cultivate, devote to God,—
Quarry bright gems from darkest mine,
Chisel till heaven-born lusters shine,
Make life where barrenness once shone,
One sparkling, radiant, zodiac, zone
Of shining virtues, to adorn
The ages distant and unborn !
They who, in league with moral ease,
Their deity, themselves, to please,
Loud, deprecating evermore,
Great planting of New England's shore,
By men of inmost heavenly mould,
Whose mission Truth, not gems, nor gold,
High Heaven to honor, earth to light,
Win back from dark, foul pagan night,
May deep complain, embarrassed feel,

Scoff, scorn devotion, faith, true zeal,
Have inward risings, qualms and pain,
At the proud advent of a reign
'Neath which shall fall each tyrant chain;
Taunt, stigmatize with lewd, vile jeer
The grandest triumphs of the sphere.
But what were man but hope forlorn,
Were no great moral sages born,
Sailing vast deeps, thought-seas of time,
Bearing great principles sublime,
Breaking all chains from bondaged mind,
Creating virtues, tastes refined,
Shaping a world, from error free,
Place underprops 'neath liberty,
Gild with opinions, maxims wise,
Drop sweet, supernal, beauteous dyes,
Re-tone the ages' throbbing life,
Give peace, true rest from endless strife?
The noblest champions of the race,
Great men of sinew, who dare face
Vile devils with their hideous stare,
Who gnash and rage and curse and swear;—
Though Hell burn hot, for Right declare,
Their ease, their pleasure dare forego,

Dark, damning systems to o'erthrow,
Confront dark power's maligning glance,
On its vile works prepared t' advance,
'Mid storms, dread hurricanes that rise,
Their steadfast gaze on Glory's prize!
When farthest pole with thunder shakes,
When earth, upheaved with earthquakes,
    quakes,
All furious tempests 'round thick blown,
Vast mighty pillars, tossed, o'erthrown,
Wild ruin's shadows falling far,
Hope, hope deep-veiled, dim, distant star;
When all foundations, riven, shake,
And granite ribs of nature break,
Convulsions, discord far and near,
Rend the long rent dissolving sphere,
They who 'mid deepening woe, distress,
Heroic dare the race to bless,
Drown'd honor save, new treasures find,
Great crushing century wrongs unbind,
Live Benefactors of mankind,—
Their life, their character, their fame,
Glory illumes, wafts, wafts their name!
Thus the great Pilgrims whom we trace,

Whose memory Time gives deepening grace,
Whose influence widening far extends,
Unspent, to unborn ages tends,
Transforming all things, giving tone,
Hushing earth's piteous, dolorous groan ;
They millions hail amid their woes,
Their beacon-guide, 'mid Fate's dark throes!
In no false mask were they e'er seen,—
A Damasc' blade, sharp, bright and keen,
They wield, Heaven's truth,—pierce error
      through,
Create grand civilizations new
Of Glory, Power, of spotless Fame,
Light, light the earth with central flame,—
Effulgent, radiant, streaming bright,
O'er all wild realms of barbarous night!
They struggle!—Life 'gainst death they wage,
Death that long masked had trod the stage
In myriad shapes of false disguise,
Bewilderment to human eyes;
Ideas false round Time had flung,
False epics coined, grim, wildly sung,
From ages sighs and groans had wrung;
The great organic structures proud,

Wrapped in its cramping, mouldering shroud,
Church, State, the grand, great common weal
Shrivelled by its all-blasting seal;
Entering all avenues of power,
To mar, devastate, spoil, devour;
Rearing arched universe of woe,
Sunless, starless, where flowers ne'er grow,
Where Desolation's empire reigns
In shadow, sackcloth, darkening chains,
Empire of horror wreathed with fire,
Combusting passions, demon ire,
Rolling in torrent wrath amain,
O'er one vast scene of deepening pain,
Dirged by laments, deep groans and sighs,
Earth's gloom unlit by sacrifice:—
Where tempest, thunder, lightnings break,
God's awful silence dismal make,
Creation trembling at its doom,
Sinking to find oblivion's tomb,
Black vortex where pollutions rot,
Fate's urn yielding no happy lot!
Such, such the moral trend of things
While ruled false right Divine of kings,
Dark tyrannies, in unchecked sway,

Sucking man's life-blood fast away,
One awful night of blackening fold,
Man for vile pottage, barter sold;
Rifled, despoiled through centuries long,
His nature crushed by gilded wrong.
Such was the stage the Pilgrims trod,
Sandalled in Truth, waving its rod,
They put their trust, their hope in God.
When for vast service they were pressed,
State, Church, by wickedness oppressed,
Called to appear before the world
With blazoning emblems high unfurled,
Glimpsing their aspect, lo! behold
A conqueror's presence, heaven enrolled;—
A form Herculean in might,
A spirit purged in purging light,
Eye steady deepening in its gaze,
Darting resistless, conquering rays,
Erect, upright, self-poised, serene,
Example, pattern, void of spleen,
Of bold, uncompromising air,
Port, mien such as great heroes wear;
In manhood panoplied complete,
Piercing hypocricies, deceit,

Grave, sober, dignified, a saint,
With no hysteric, soft complaint,
Exact, prompt, rigorous, just, true,
Of vast, wide, comprehending view,
Life's being with a rising star
Of greatness, glory, beaming far,—
Conventionalisms from weakness sprang,
Spurned by a gruff, deep, nasal twang,
No pretty follies of the day
Allowed in life's stupendous play,—
Deep sense of truth, high, holy, calm,
With daily food of prayer and psalm;—
Drinking Truth's nectar,—gems they wear,
Its hues supernal, changeless, fair,
Its shining bracelets, bands of gold,
Imperial purples, fold on fold,
Embroidered by immortal art;
Their conscience pure, of spotless heart:—
They wear Truth's sash, of scarlet shade,
In flaming tassels, golden braid,
Its em'rald scarf 'round shoulders flung,
With golden fringes beauteous hung,
Endiadem'd in Truth supreme,
They wear its sword whose edges gleam,

Its hilt of diamond, point keen fire,
Whose waving circles worlds inspire,
Its outleap from its scabbard's glow
Doom to the mightiest marshalled foe,
With halberd, lance, bright, glittering spear,
Mightier than knight, than chevalier,
Prince, king, with their false, borrowed fame,
Hereditary titles,—name,
Than laurelled chieftains, whose dark crest
Proclaims a world abject, oppressed,—
Sage, prophet, priest, hero combined,
The flower consummate of mankind,
Abating dire temptation's thorn,
Perfection's parentage first born,
In radiant plumes, broad-waving, grand,
By Heaven's sweet haloes bright o'erspanned ;
In thought profound, deep, sagely scanned,
With beaming brow, Truth's lifted hand,
On whose forefinger flashed sublime
The brightest diamond of all time !
Full armored, breastplated with light,
Prepared, when God signals the fight,
To battle for man's great birth-right
On any soil beneath the sun,

Where glory, honor's prize are won!
Accouter'd thus in Heavenly grace,
Hero of heroes in Time's race,
'Neath Truth's bright shield, with glittering
    mace,
The Pilgrim, sworn earth's wrongs t' erase,
Goes forth, stands in the cooling breeze,
Surveys the lands, the sunlit seas,
His presence symbol of Heaven's light,
Whose charm dissolves creation's night!
No warrior of the bloody creed,
Yet power by which mankind is freed;
Dark carnal weapons laid aside,
Yet spreading victories far and wide,—
God's new, grand miracle sublime,
A presence 'mid these realms of time,
At whose appearance life re-spheres,
New orbs unveil, new sun appears,
The stars in new-born luster shine,
Garlands celestial bright entwine,
Radiance, new beauty, walk the earth,
New splendors fall, as at Time's birth,
The shadows turned all crimsoning glow,
Dark Desolation's aged woe

Transformed, with loveliness o'erspread,
Life plucks the scepter, death is dead!
Far through the world's august domain,
Decks a bright empire's coming reign,—
The earth uncrowned, in travail heaves,
Rich tassels bud for golden sheaves,
Life lifts new arch, in glory spanned,
With corridors receding, grand,
Forelighting farthest future land,
Bright pillar, column, shining tower,
Draperied in light, its beauteous flower,
Gemm'd, tassell'd, wove, all rich, inwrought
With emblems of transcending thought,
Flashing sweet lusters in a blaze
Of glory's beauty-wedded rays,
Falling wide o'er the rescued earth,
An Eden's dawn in second birth.
Through that proud arch nations now move
In deepening harmonies of love,
In thoughtful, meditative mood,
Planning the world's enduring good;
The North, the South, the East, the West,
All lands with thronging footsteps pressed,
Vieing to reach a common goal,

Where Life's pure streams of crystal roll :—
Life,—not where bubbles burst in air,
Devoid of labor, pains and care,—
Life,—not of pomp, of pageants trim,
Of fantasies, caprice and whim,
Of roistering jargon, base retreat,
Of balderdash, of froth, deceit,
Of fripperies, worthlessness complete,—
But Life of thought, of living soul,
Of enterprise of wide control,
Of movements that inspire with awe,
The Life of Order, Grandeur, Law!
Would man obtain that sovereign prize,
Life's beauteous boon that distant lies,
Its crowning honors, grand estate,
Be named among the wise and great,
The rose of memory on his tomb,
In fragrant, rich, perennial bloom?
In Mayflowers he must sail all seas,
Fearless of storms, the deadening breeze,
Steer where Avatar never trod,
His shield, defence, hope, trust, in God;
Gird on the armor of Heaven's Truth,
Pursue the toil from dawn of youth

7

Till manhood, age, creep on apace,
Nor then e'er think to yield the race;
Fearless of dangers, perils dire,
Of dungeons, torments, martyr fire,
Learning through sacrifice supreme
Where falls Heaven's brightest, richest beam,
That 'tis on Duty's path, well run,
Shall rise God's never-setting sun,
Each pilgrimage, early and late,
Ending where swings Heaven's pearl-bright
    gate!
He who the energies of Life
Consumes in struggles, glorious strife,
Wrestling for Truth, its spotless fame,
To vindicate, advance its claim,
Enduring want, e'er scorning ill,
Time's grandest destinies to fill,
Working, waiting, courageous still;
Through hero conquests he shall rise,
Eternal triumph in the skies,
With harp of light on sea of gold,
Be with the sons of light enrolled!
Thus would the muse pursue her strain,
Weave in sweet numbers, golden chain,

Bind brows with garland-wreaths of fame,
Glimpse destinies of heavenly name,
Stirring the slumbering souls that lie
Unmoved in self-idolatry,
Till fired with resolution,—zeal,
They through their inmost natures feel
Rousing to action, grand, sublime,
Like Pilgrims go and garland Time.
The Pilgrims, chosen host of God,
When o'er the stormy, raging flood
They rear Time's mighty pillar grand,
Darting effulgence for each land,
Each ebb and flow of their great soul
Pointing to Freedom's glowing goal,
The adamantine chains unbind,
Come scenes of grandeur, sweet, refined,
New rising orbs the shadows chase,
The world bright flowers in Light's embrace,
Anathemas o'ertake each ill,
Omnipotent the People's will!
O ! who can tell from joys begun
What mightier triumphs shall be won,
When from the human path is rolled
Each lingering wrong, each curse of old,

When pangs of sorrow, throbbing grief,
Pains, agonies, find full relief;
When from the marge, the widening sphere
Of human nature, dries each tear,
Propitious power with genial hand
Exile dark tyrants from each land,—
Supplant vile outrage, base command,
Give pledges, shelter, safety grand;
And man erect in Freedom stand,—
Time's deepening course shall grow divine,
Truth's full-orbed constellations shine;
Pure, sweet, all holy, precious, rare,
The Pilgrim fruitage Time shall bear.
Mayflowers enwrapped in tempests dark,
The foundering, crumbling, Pilgrim bark
Shall gem with earth's immortal spark,
Bloom roseate, waft sweet fragrance far,
Be hailed 'neath every sun and star,
Perfume the world with incense sweet,
Crown Plymouth Rock high Glory's seat!
Aye, Plymouth Rock, ice-clad, frost-bound,
Yet flinging fire, a world around,—
The fire of thought, of changeless Truth,—
In garlands of perennial youth.

A rock from which white beam of light
Darts and dissolves the centuries' night;
A rock of power, imperial, grand,
Whose lodestar touch builds every land;
That changes Time, remodels man,
In civilization leads the van.
A rock where gush pure founts of Life,
Healing the world's long maddening strife;
Whose living current's onward flow,
Hurl tyrannies in overthrow,
A mystic, philosophic stone!
By which mankind renewed, are won
To Virtue, Order, Truth and Law,
Flaming like that the Prophet saw;
Turning to gold, creation's prize,
Before which damning error dies!
While Time those champions e'er shall greet,
Its mighty work they urge, complete,
Their name, immortal deeds shall sound ,--
Rouse, rouse the vast creation round,
Grow watchword fire each patriot heart,
As nations rise,—from bondage start;
'Mid oppressed lands, long bleeding, torn,
Defying tyranny with scorn ;—

Through them shall rise a lineage grand,
Their name be great, with Glory spanned,
Tracing all deeps, ploughing the earth,
Immortal seed give quickening birth!
Tossing to air the fabrics old,
Laying foundations bright with gold,—
Th' embattled masonry of Time
Re-raise, with monuments sublime.
Their glorious standard traced with Right,
Waving in folds of deepening light,
Upborne, advanced, high through the earth
Shall come, enthroning man's great birth;
Of Power, of Destiny, of Fame,
No more a scorned, an outcast name.
Endiadem'd his head shall peer,—
High-priest of Nature,—through her sphere;
Lord of creation's vast domain,
With equal power to serve or reign!
Then shall the world,
Long tossed and whirled,
See its proud period grand;
A mighty day,
Purging away
The mists from every land.

In joy, in pride,
Then side by side,
Shall walk the lowly, great,
Title nor rank
Man's right outflank,
In Time's true modelled state!
Wars cease their rage,
Carnage engage
Ambition, Power, no more,—
Distil sweet balm,
The world's great calm,
Peace reign on every shore!
The living ties,—
Dear amities,—
Strong bind the sundered race;
In concords sweet
Great ages meet,
New blushing glories trace!
Vast Jubilee
From land and sea
Shall roll its thunders round,
Pealing afar,
'Neath every star,
The hemispheres around .

Then midnight specters, shades shall sweep,
Sink in oblivion's wakeless sleep,
Enchantment thrill,—Time's anguish, pain
Return no more,—a holy reign
Of righteousness, of heavenly joy,
Of Love, good will, without alloy,
Shall lift all heavenly symbols bright
O'er Time's dissolved, tempestuous night;
Columns of Glory pierce the skies,
Songs, benedictions, thundering rise,
Re-echoed from each distant shore,
The nations freed, their God adore!

PART II.

—

Warmed, fired with eulogistic strain,
For Pilgrims, sailing through the main,
Say, mighty Muse, what brought them o'er,
To plant New England's icy shore?
What quenchless fires within them burn,
That thither they their footsteps turn,
Resistless make, fearless, and bold,
Meek worshipers in God's true fold?
What raised their souls, chastised, so high,—
Heroic made when perils nigh,—
Winged them with flame of Seraphim,
Gave pinions of proud Cherubim,
Strength for their hour, grand race to run,
Lighted by rays from Glory's sun?
Bright, bright examples for the race,—
Their influence lives, nor can efface,
Immortal, quickening, e'er to climb,

Pervade the world of being, Time,
Crown all with destinies sublime!
When nature's birth the angels sung,
And heavenly spheres their chimes outrung;
When Beauty robed the new-made world,
And Time's great signal lights unfurled,
Then man in youthful morning's prime
Went forth, began his course sublime,
Sovereign of earth, creation's Lord,
Unmarred his peace, unsheathed the sword,—
Gazing, earth smiled a paradise,—
His portion joy, abounding bliss;
With rapture's sway, ecstatic thrill,
His senses all his passions fill;
The present full of sweet delight,
Walking 'mid deepening splendors bright!
Not thus his race unbroken sped,
On endless bounties, dainties fed,
All prospects ravishing his eye,
While energies in slumber lie;
Dark omens his horizon, far
Around, dim his rising star;
Portents of ill, thicken, combine,
Force Past to Future to resign,—

Eclipsed all lights, but dimly shine,
Fair buds, fair blossoms,—flowers divine,—
Fade, fade the garland wreaths, that twine;
The present solace flung away,
To gild some distant future day,
When triumph, rapture, joy, new praise,
O'er sorrow, gloom, sweet songs shall raise.
Lo! traveller 'mid a desert strand,
Far, far, a mountain rises grand,
Dim-veiled, yet roseate in the light
Of morn's new-waking splendors bright;
Where peaceful cot, proud palace fair,
Glint through the enfoliaged, scented air,—
Vast interspaces lying drear,
For battle, conflict, doubt and fear;
Dark moanings from the charnell'd dead,
Starting the stoutest souls with dread,—
Unearthly sounds, hideous to scare,
Wierd spectral terrors lurking there;—
Through sunless passes forced to go,
Baffled, oft checked, his passage slow,
Oft slain by Fancy's conjured foe,
Fearing each step rout, overthrow;
That mountain cheers, its sunbeams play

Inspires him mid his rugged way,
Strengthens his step the race to run,
Till goal of light, of rest, be won !
Thus Faith, amid Time's woful fall,
A Heaven-born power can disenthral,
Uplifts, inspires, makes vigorous, strong,
To battle 'gainst assailing wrong,
Endure all struggles, fierce and long,
Pointing to summits in the skies,
Where robed in light its mansion lies !
Nature may shine, in gorgeous light,
Her suns soon set in dismal night ;
Joys, joys of life, this day began,
May end in woe to mortal man ;
The sweetest solace of each hour
Darken with torment's endless power !
Why should not fear, dark terror, mock,
Man's bark oft wrecked on ruin's rock,—
The cresting billows' roaring play
Unnerve, take all his strength away,
He powerless on his course to lie,
Mere floating waif on waters high,
Whose thunderous, surging, tumbling roll,
Shakes to equator, farthest pole ;

Startled by every piercing sound,
Dashed fugitive, creation round!
See man a feather, blown through air,
Seeking false rest in Vanity Fair,—
Proud child of deep parental care,
Given to God in Chrism, prayer;
Of powers immortal, essence rare,
In Heavenly glories made to share;—
A spirit all of quenchless fire,
To live when nature, worlds, expire,
Can he find rest, contentment here,
Within this narrow, curtained sphere,
Cramped and hemmed in by fettering Force—
By partial views, without resource
For his winged spirit, deathless mind,
To nature finite unresigned,
Struggling to rise and bound away,
Where his vast powers can freely play,
Expand, unfold, e'er upward climb,
Next to his Maker grand, sublime?
Auspicious Faith! eternal Hope!
While Time drinks all man's spirits up,
Thou, Thou alone canst point the way
In which his mortal feet ne'er stray.

Proud denizen of no mean fold,
Vast flaming essence, high enrolled
With sons of Light, Heaven's streets of gold
To walk, in proud celestial mien,
Immortal victor yet be seen,
'Mid triumph's august light serene;
Thou, Thou alone canst guide his course,
From vanity, from sin, remorse,
Disclose green pastures of delight,
Give prospects ravishing to sight
Of things nor eye nor ear have known
In this low vale, with thorns o'ergrown;
Of wondrous treasures fair that lie
Secure in immortality,—
Where spirits, brightening as they go,
Of bliss partake to overflow;
Of pangs, of sorrows, never know,
Passing beyond all bounds of woe;
A happy throng in triumph's flight
Gazing on Beatific Light,—
Their purging vision waxing bright,
Entranced, enraptured as they rise,
Find thought in endless, sweet surprise,
In each of which a Heaven lies!

Almighty Faith ! Life to the soul
Sojourning where Time's waters roll,—
Primeval Daughter of the skies,
Each, every terrene ill, defies.
The darkest cloud it gilds with Light,
Enstars the starless gloom of night,—
Round threatening storms of direful woe,
It spans Heaven's radiant, matchless bow ;—
Earthquakes may heave, rocks fiercely rend,
Colossal Force its wrath expend,
Convulsions dire upheave a world,
Black ruin's missiles round he hurled,
Lit by Faith's radiant beaconing star,
No ill can touch, no danger mar,
Heaven's omnipresence safe e'er guides,
Man's fragile bark peril outrides,
Light breaks ahead, all glorious, grand,
'Till reached the goal, each promised land !
Thus were great patriarchs ancient led,
Through scenes where sorrows dire o'erspread
Darkness before them like a wall,
Creation wrapt in sablest pall,—
Avenging fiends, terrific foes,
Concocting tribulations, woes,

Defeat, disaster, ruin, rout,
Gins, traps, snares, pitfalls spread about !
Lo ! as they yield to beckoning Time,
Go forth on pilgrimage sublime,
Heaven's brightness falls about their head,
Fair, beauteous landscapes wide outspread,
Heroic, valiant, is their tread ;
Sweet deserts smile in lovely bloom,
Each threatening foe appalled makes room,
The hostile nations meet their doom ;
Dissolve the glooms of terror's night,
Transcending omens charm their sight,
Their journeyings brighten 'neath God's
        light,
Effulging, burning, radiant, bright:—
Proud champions to duty true,
They cut their way triumphant through,—
O'ercome the obstacles they meet,
'Mid fragrant incense rising sweet,—
Their labors close, with visions greet,
Behold redemption's tragic seat,—
From Pisgah's mountain summits gaze,
See Canaan smile 'neath Glory's blaze !
Primeval Faith ! when Adam fell

Say, what the rapture of thy spell;
When Eden closed on mortal sight,
Thou, thou didst give the wanderers light;
Turned from those fair Elysian bowers,
To track this blasted world of ours,
Where woe, disaster, rushed apace,
And toil and suffering crown the race;
Where every form of human ill
Dire sorrow's cup were left to fill,
A bitter portion, human life,
Embittering envies, feuds, and strife,
Contentions, discords, fierceness, rife,
No solace, friendship, left behind,
With balm the spirit bruised to bind;
Thou from God's throne, effulgent, bright,
Didst dart thy beams, through nature's night;
'Midst murder, war, dread famine, pain,
Didst trace an Eden lost to gain,
In distant spheres, point out repose,
Supernal, 'yond life's transient woes,
Its dizzying day-dreams, falseness, shame,
Dire disappointments, airy fame,
Its griefs, its melancholy, care,
Vain glitterings pomps, false pageant's glare,

Its meteor lights, their changing gleam,
Its emptiness, bubble supreme;
Bid man desponding lift his head,
Re-kindle hope forever fled;
Heaven's closed portals didst unbar,
And light the path to Glory there!
Immortal Faith! Eternal Power!
On rock of adamant they tower
Who seize thy wand, erect and free,
Go forth for God, man, Liberty!
Joined in communion with the skies,
Earth's treacheries, hindrance, they outrise,
See with new sense, illumined eyes,
The vast, immutable, unknown,
Heaven's high, august, eternal throne,
Sweet choirs angelic, spiritual, bright,
Great forms effulgent robed in light,
Intelligences raying fire,
Who from the Infinite ne'er retire!
Encircling hosts that towering rise,
All radiant through immortal skies,
Pealing Hosanna's anthem strain,
Echoing in deepening, sweet refrain,
Immortal as Jehovah's reign!

All high, all low, all vast, profound,
The universe, unveiled, around,
All heights, all depths, relations, spanned,
All systems by the Almighty planned,
Creative Power, in depths, in height,
Great forces blind, marshalled for Right,
The elements at war around,
In seeming discord, wild, unbound,
Yet order, harmony, delight,
While systems endless wheel their flight;
Center, circumference, everywhere,
But portions of one guardian care!
Beneath Faith's star, in gloomiest night
Man walks by sure, unerring light;
An heavenly beam illumes his way,
Flung from the realms of endless day;
Forebodings fly, assuages fear,
The path of duty, life, grows clear;
All things, in harmony, rejoice,
Speak with select, inspiring voice;
Where'er is life, where'er is soul,
Pure nectar-founts gush, sweetly roll,
By day, by night, in endless round,
Love's melodies, sweet songs resound.

In peace, in triumph, love and joy,
Earth's myriads move, no base alloy
To mar, upset, quench the sweet light,
Turn noon-tide into starless night;
No jarring discords, grating noise,
To drown the accents Faith employs;
Its diapasons, endless chime,
Rolling in melodies sublime,
Hymning God's works, His ways profound,
The universe turns hallowed ground;
Starting, an endless race to run,
Man feels, through Faith, triumph begun!
Faith, 'tis the grand, immortal tie;
It brings omnipotencies nigh,
Heaven's strength imparts its sovereign power,
Man hero makes in peril's hour;
The surging seas, all boist'rous deeps,
He braves,—his course still onward keeps,
The foaming, thundering, roaring flood
Submissive to his guardian God;
Storms, tempests, in their utmost rage,
For him a hand divine engage,
Tornadoes, simoons, whirlwinds dire,
Great hurricanes, devouring fire,

Fierce, plunging torrents, nerve, inspire;—
The elements to madness driven,
Lo! then he puts his trust in Heaven;
And should the mountains, valleys quake,
Nature, convulsed in terror, shake,
Earth's central forces onset make,
Passion's wild fiend-fire, horrid, break,
Dark, vile ambition, ply the stake,
Earth, hell, all innocence o'ertake,
No cooling draughts man's thirst to slake,
Heaven once engaged can ne'er forsake!
Faith, of all graces grandest, fair,
On Heaven bids man e'er cast his care,
Illumed by its eternal beam,
Lo! feebleness becomes supreme;—
The clouds of sense dissolve, pass by,
Innoxious clears the storm-rent sky,
The threat'ning violences cease,
E'en Hell proclaims a truce of peace;—
Each votary walks serene and calm,
Where tempests rage drop scents of balm.
The boasting, proud, lose the bright crown,
The weak wax strong, win high renown,
The laurelled great, doubt, stumble, fall,—

Faith's votary triumphs over all,
In Heaven's eternal counsel, plan,
Ordained to lead the centuries' van,
Open great human pathway bright,
'Mid fragrance, bloom, Heaven's deep'ning
    light!
Unequal to the tasks of Time,—
See feeble man dare deeds sublime,
Go forth at duty's sovereign call,
Heaven's smile his shield, protection wall,—
Pursue high course, run bright career,
For spotless Fame, true Glory, steer;
Fearless in Right's great cause engage,
Meeting dire foes, subdue their rage,
With deepening luster star Time's page,
O'ercome antagonisms, wrong,
Darkness of ages, dense and strong;
Great altars light, vile tyrants shame,
Conquer, and win great hero name!
'Twas in that Faith the Pilgrims came,
With souls of fire, with hearts of flame;
The path of ages opened bright,
'Mid battling tempest, gloom and night.
In virtues strong, their graces fair,

In qualities heroic, rare,
On Heaven's eternal rock of Truth,
When Plymouth's fades to shine in youth,
They lay foundations, mightier, grand,
Than were through ancient centuries planned;
Foundations whence shall glorious rise
Proud structures, when all terrene dies,
Fling wide their bulwarks, open door,
Where light's deep tides in silence pour,
Send pinnacles in glory bright,
Peering through all these realms of night,
Flashing sweet radiance, heavenly light;
Splendors to deepen, far unseal,
Immortal tablatures reveal,
Grand architectures for the skies,
Prepare high Heaven societies;
Illustrious bands, by Faith made strong,
To roll celestial airs along,
Stir the deep flame, that seraphs feel,
While Heaven's eternal anthems peal!
For what grand purpose do they come,
O'er midnight seas compelled to roam?
They come 'mid perils, deep distress,
All future time to lighten bless;

To chase all fears and doubts away,
The world's long anguish, gloom, dismay.
Their pilgrimage, a priceless boon,
Great morn empurpling on high noon,
All roseate, waxing heavenly bright,
Flooding all bounds with glorious light.
They come to build new, sweet, sweet home,
By Christ's dear church, its flashing dome,
For Love's pure, sweetest honey-comb,
For nectar's sparkle, brightest foam,
Mount Satan's imps, yet never clomb,
A budding height, undimmed by gloom,
Sweet fount of Life 'mid living bloom,
A weedless garden for the Lord,
Where Heaven's great king shall be adored.
Time's sweetest relic 'mid the fall,
The Eden state's fairest recall,
Darkened, made desolate and wild,
By pagans, savage, nature's child:—
Enclosure grand, sweet pride of earth,
Where human nature at its birth
First breathes the vital, balmy air,
Begins Life's consciousness to share,
They deck, adorn, make spotless bright,

Youth's, manhood's, age's sweet delight,—
Enshrine with innocence and Love,
'Neath Heaven's ministries above,
Sweet shelter from the blasting storm,
Where earliest plans and prospects form,
Where as Life robes in purple bloom,
Sheds its enriching sweet perfume,
All energies that there unfold,
In virtue's cause to be enrolled,
Each flowering young immortal mind,
To Heaven's high service be assigned,
Life's purpose, aims, its hopes, its all,
An offering ready at Heaven's call,—
The family, true social state,
They dignify, high elevate,—
Make fountain-head, there high to rise,
Life's waters, as the fount supplies;—
Proud castle, fortress,—safe retreat,
'Gainst which in vain Sin's billows beat,—
Perfection's shrine, its chosen seat,—
There all that quickens, nerves, inspires,
To kindle beaming altar-fires,
All chastening emblems there to lie,
Lust, outrage, wrong, base pride defy;—

No guileful passions entering there,
Life's innocence, its bliss, to share,—
Symbols of excellence divine,
All virtues heavenly pure to shine,
Unfading garland wreaths entwine;
All radiant gems from God's bright mine,
Ray their sweet luster, quenchless beam,
Make concord, happiness, supreme.
There the first paths of life to fill,
With order, true submissive will,
Obedience, reverence, faith, Heaven's Truth,
The grandest ornaments of youth,—
Grandeur, magnificence, true power,
To star each nascent, forming hour,
The child, no waif cast dark abroad,
But pregnant with the fires of God,
Vast, slumbering charm, to quicken, rise,
The ages warm, then star the skies!
Love's center, where new growths surprise,
Where friendship's kindled altars stand,
With grace, true culture, overspanned,
Where being's wants find full supply,
Life darting its immortal dye,
Angels in throngs with minstrelsy

Harping to Heaven's Eternal King,
They home's pure glories ceaseless sing!
With thoughts thus raised, uplifted, grand,
See them with giants plant a land,—
No puny dwarfs,—no drivelling clan,
But demigods, superior man,—
A race gigantic in its might,
To battle in the cause of Right;
Great Pilgrim stock, of lineage rare,
Ordained the centuries' load to bear,
Rousing the nations from their sleep,
To gaze and wonder o'er the deep,—
Foremost to watch, to work, and plan,
Great champion guides, leading Time's van,
Whose flag is now on every wave,
Fearless, upright, victorious, brave!
Say, mighty Muse, home, country dear,
Falls not for motherland a tear?
Heaves not some inward groan, a sigh,
At glorious mem'ries, grand and high,
Distinctions, grandeur, glory, fame,
That fadeless wreathe Britannia's name?
There 'mid wild tossings, darkened Time
They Magna Chartas read, sublime;

Long generations, as they toil,
See bloodiest tyrants rend, despoil;
Earth's mightiest genius' blazing star
Burst midnight gloom, fling sunbeams far;
Great Shakspeare, Bacon, Milton, rise,
Pour cheering light on mortal eyes;
Time's matchless champions, heroes grand,
Who proud ameliorations planned,—
Defenders of eternal Right,
Amid monarchic, tyrant night!
But woe, alas! for them in vain
Their star guides o'er the heaving main,—
A liberty for them in store
Nor man, nor ages, knew before;—
Vast Power, whose safeguards Time shall
    feel,
As tyrants quake, and thrones shall reel,—
Heaven's winged, bright, beaming radiant
    form,
Peering, 'mid sunshine, through the storm,
Man, Justice, Right, waxing supreme,
At touch of its enstarring beam;—
Lo! they behold their sweet delight,
Its orb here rising grandly bright;

Gazing, their sovereign God adore,
Plant its bright ensigns 'long the shore,
Forget the ignominies past,
Their future hopes here anchor fast.
Baptized with Freedom's glowing fire,
No·other land now wakes desire;
England the old fades from their view,
They consecrate an England new,
To man's God-given, eternal right,
To come no more dark, tyrant night;
Vast destinies to break in light,
Truth wax triumphant over might;
Here the proud love great martyr's feel,
A deathless flame, through them to steal!
Their past experience they review,
God's providence e'er guiding true,
Retrace their steps when 'mid the sea
They sought new lands, homes for the free!
Repass their voyages o'er again,
Listening to ocean's grand refrain;
As thoughts fast rise, spread golden wing,
Farewell's they to their country sing:

THE PILGRIM'S FAREWELL SONG.

Adieu! adieu! England, adieu!
Blest native land adieu! adieu!
With cheers we spread the bending sail,
And ride before the driving gale;
Home we leave, to Heaven resigned,
Leave our land we love behind!

We spurn to be the tyrant's thrall,
Whate'er dark destiny befall;
Our God will be our sovereign Guide,
Conduct us safe o'er waters wide,—
Breath of heaven waft us far,
'Neath high heaven's e'er guiding star!

Though billows plunge our fragile bark,
With dallying sport, 'mid tempests dark,
The ocean tremble to its bed,
Swift, forkéd lightnings round be sped,
Till each sailor heart shall bow,
Fearing ocean's depths to plough;

With hearts upright we'll onward go,
Ye mighty tempests, fiercer blow,
Ne'er, ne'er will we consent to be

Where mind immortal is not free,—
Free to worship God with prayer,
Free to think, to do, and dare!

Sweet, clarion voices greet our ear,
Sounds musical through storms we hear,
Prophetic lights about us burn,
Glimmer, as west our faces turn;
Soon our labors will be o'er,
Footsteps press a happier shore!

A brighter land, lo! bursts amain,
Sweet land for Freedom's holier reign,
Land of the pine, magnolia, palm,
Where skies are blue and air is balm,
Land of sweet, of happy rest,
Land for exiles sore oppressed!

'Tis proud Columbia, glorious, fair,—
We come her hills, her vales to share,
Her virgin soil plant for the race
With mighty germs to burst apace;
'Till, with splendor streaming wide,
She, of lands, shall be earth's pride!

The wilderness shall bud with charms,
Tossing to Heaven its giant arms,
Nature's imperial, grand retreat,
Shall yet be empire's grandest seat,

Art and Science here shall bloom.
Truth eternal waft perfume!

Here, while the centuries roll their round,
For man shall this be hallowed ground,
The mountain and the ocean strand
Be joined in Freedom's wedlock band,
Man to worship God be free,
Heir of Heaven-born liberty!

Here altars pure shall brightly burn,
No despot human nature spurn,
Hard bondage, want, be known no more,
Heaven's bounteous blessings endless pour;
Here we make our anchors fast,
Firm, secure, the deep o'erpassed!

Let anthem-strains to Heaven's high King,
Loud, land and sea in tribute bring;
Through His Almighty, guiding hand,
Breaks on our view the promised land!
Adieu! adieu! England, adieu!
Homes we love, adieu! adieu!

Ah! who can tell how heaves the sigh,
When forced to bid the last good-bye;
The shrine of home, its sweets to leave,
Where memories fondest garlands weave,
Give the last parting, lingering glance,

On unknown perils, toils, advance,
Leave all to true affection dear,
For distant suns, another sphere.
Country! dear native land! what thought
With magnet, lodestar power, so fraught!
It wakes our being's inmost fires,
Stirs holiest Love, warms, thrills, inspires,
Flings radiance o'er the path of Time,
Enwreathes in haloes grand, sublime;
Whether where tropic heats and bloom
Yield fairest flowers of sweet perfume,
Where purple golden lusters bright,
Festooned in beauty, charm, delight,
Delicious fruits, the annual year,
Ripen as in some Eden's sphere;—
Whether 'mid temperate zones and air,
Where culture prompts to labors rare,
Where toiling man, in thoughtful mood,
With beading brow secures his food,
Or 'mid fierce Arctic's driving snows,
Unblest with lily's smile, or rose,
Where tempests howl with deafening roar,
And icebergs crash along the shore,—
Where night appals with lengthening gloom,

Unlit save by Aurora's bloom ;
Howe'er secluded, lone, it lay,
Far from the thronged, the beaten way
Of mortal men, whose tides e'er pour,
And touch each monumented shore !
Deep, deep within the home-bred heart,
For Country, what emotions start !
'Tis like a charm, a potent spell,
A wave of nectar, at whose swell
Man tastes of pure, Elysian bliss,
Of rapture's thrilling happiness,—
Quaffs deep, sweet fountains of delight,
His morning star all radiant, bright !
Turning it o'er and o'er again,
Of orphanage who dare complain,
That Time is but an empty reign
Of darkness, and the tyrant chain,
Life, a grim cheat, a phantom vain,
Naught solid, true here e'er to gain,—
Delusion, lie of deepest stain,
And shall forever thus remain,—
Country ! its image soothes our pain,
Gives back the loved to Life again,
Its pleasure-songs, its triumph strain,

Immortalizing heroes slain !
Its thronging memories crowding start,
Thrill with electric fire each heart,
Renew rare deeds. great glories vast,
Tell how long generations past
The fathers breathed this fitful life,
Plunged in great conflicts, glorious strife,
Through toils, through banishments, here won
The boon whence all our life-streams run,—
Through pain, through poverty, despair,
Made us the beings that we are ;—
How, when misfortune's hurricanes blew,
They to their God, to Duty true,
For long posterity, want, shame,
Endured, to waft true Glory,—Fame!
With martyrdoms, with groans, with sighs,
With tears, with blood, with agonies,
Reared the proud structures that we see,
The star-domed shrines of Liberty !
Grand forms majestic throng unseen,
Illustrious, godlike in their mien ;
Great sages, heroes, they who drew
Bold maxims from deep fountains new,
Before whose lifted radiant shield,

Barbaric legions quailed and reeled,
Snatched victory from black ruin's jaws,
To Chaos, Anarchy, gave laws,—
Society ordained, gave peace,
Content, joy, happiness,
Prosperities that nations crown,
Rights that enstar, give high renown,
Ending barbaric vengeance, crime,
Twining with wreaths the brow of Time!
A presence august folds us round,
We tread on sacred, hallowed ground,—
New impulse, vigor, through us steal,
A deepening consciousness we feel.
Of manoood, of true patriot joy,
Those ties Time, distance, ne'er destroy.
New well-springs, fountains, in us rise;
These are our own, our native skies!
Here Heaven flings wide cerulean arch,
As on Time's pilgrimage we march;
Sun, moon, and stars, the rainbowed sky,
Shed benedictions from on high,
Dew-drops that sparkle on earth's breast,
The larks' gay carol, give us rest;
The sunshine, storm, with garlands twine,

In brightness, beauty, all things shine;
The land, the deep, great ocean's swell,
In diapason, thunder, tell;
Here boyhood played with sportive air,
Here sacred lips taught our first prayer,
Stern Duty's hallowed precepts gave,
Re-hearsed the story of the brave ;
Taught us temptation e'er to fly,
For Honor live, for Glory die !
Country ! sweet Home ! their living cheer,
To true-born hearts how grateful, dear ;—
The velvet lawn, the buds that swell,
Sweet waterfall, the woodland dell,
The merry chimes, sweet christmas bell,
The school-house, church, the glistening spire,
Rare social charms, 'round winter fire ;
Thanksgiving's mirth, true serious thought,
What endless pleasures they have brought !
'Tis there the garner'd good of life
Distils in blessings, nameless, rife,
The gifts Heaven gives fond man to know,
A pilgrim in these realms below,
Where heart finds bliss, man asks no more,
Save Heaven the Giver to adore.

Let man be tossed, by tempests hurled,
Far o'er the traveled, storied world;
Drop pilgrim tear on ancient shrine,
See dusty Grandeur garlands twine;
Walk where the sun of Glory rose
And set 'mid quick returning woes,—
'Mid fanes that still 'neath shadows rise,
The fading beams of foreign skies,
Grand monuments where stately power
Imperial shone its destined hour,—
Where pride, ambition, strove for fame,
And triumphs won that waft their name,—
Hear the dread, thundering, awful crash
Of centuries, 'mid lightning flash;
Their deep-toned, heaving, solemn dirge,
As civilizations new emerge,—
Of grander import, higher aim,
Struggling to raise mankind, reclaim,—
Hear startling avalanches fall,
Time's marshalled legions tramp and call,
As through vast revolutions dire,
Earth has re-lit her altar-fire;—
Country! its star set in the main,
Nor life nor hope can cheer again,—

Its radiant folds flung to the sky,
Man lives, nor fears when called to die;
Strong is his aim, inspired his heart,
To act some worthy hero part;
The living fires of nature warm,
He fears nor peril, conflict, storm,—
Herculean force, resistless might,
It gives to valor called to fight,
Opening the path of fortress'd Time,
Through battling energies sublime;
The mightiest pillars shaking down,
To place on man a victor crown!
What are all alien pomps and pride,
The sight of native land denied,—
Imperial splendor, gorgeousness,
Plumed royalties in courtly dress,
Grace, Fashion, in their full-orbed beam,
Magnificence, grandeur supreme;—
The lovely shrine of being, birth,
That holiest spot of all the earth,
Its star eclipsed, remediless gloom,
Enshrouding patriot, hero tomb,
Torn from warm sympathies away,
O'erthrown, no monumental ray

To tell where Greatness, Glory, won,
And man proud race victorious run;—
The robes may trail, the garlands twine,
The diamonds blaze from richest mine,
Star'd, diadem'd beauty peerless shine,
All that proud wealth, Fortune, e'er gave,
To make the monarch rival slave,—
When one's bright native star goes down,
No foreign realm can give renown;—
The heart's deep longings, hopes delayed,
All brilliance pales, wears somber shade,—
Nature, her scenes so glorious, fair,
The vales far winding, hill and air,
Earth, sea, the mountains, land and sky,
Lose all their charms, their glories die,—
A gathering darkness falls around,
Man walks no more on hallowed ground,
Is but rude wanderer, Pilgrim tossed,
His bark dashed, shattered, anchor lost,—
Driven by winds that fiercely blow,
His life-blood palsied in its flow!
Dear native land! its kindling star,
Let that but gleam, shine dim, afar,
Burst in full radiance from the cloud,

Man leaps for joy, speaks, shouts aloud,
His heart swift homeward fondly turns,
Heaven's lighted altar for him burns.
Though wandering far with pensive tread,
'Mid scenes to former glory wed,
Each distant, lonely, stranger strand
Grows kindred to his mother land;—
The shaded temple, moss-o'ergrown,
Each lonely pile, memorial stone,
The pillar'd arch, vast colonnade,
Where Fancy, musing, oft hath strayed,
The centuries bursting from their shroud,
'Mid mighty voices thundering loud,
Startling the tranced, the list'ning ear,
Ravished, immortal tales to hear;—
Let Country dart its living beam,
Its banners wave, its ensigns stream,
Roseate, encrowned with new-sprung light,
Glad day-spring's purple where was night;—
The barren heath, lone desert drear,
E'en fen, bog, morass wild, can cheer,—
Each tufted tree, the moss-decked rose,
Rock, dust, the sand, in beauty glows;
Earth's outspread scenes smile far and wide,

The mountain peaks, they tower in pride,
The smoke-wreathed vales that lie beside,
Smiling, reclothe, wear bright attire,
Again they charm, delight, inspire,
The orb of Life swells full and round,
Each land becomes sweet hallowed ground,—
Rare scenes of power, of conquest, fame,
But point to kindred blood and name!
Though checkered, diverse, one vast whole
Is human life, while ages roll;
For, whether walks he native strand,
Or roams in distant foreign land,
Man's wants, his wishes, toils, his prayer,
Spoils, triumphs, trophies, victories, care,
Are one,—one is his fated doom,
From cradle to the sheltering tomb,
Life from its kindling, embryo spark,
To where shuts round the impervious dark,
Vast mystery deep, they who have trod
Time's stage, quick back return to God!
Infinite lines, converging, draw
To one vast point of Being, law!
The farthest shores, their laving seas,
Terrestrial homes, sage, prophet sees,

Where mingling destinies 'mid night,
Prepare for realms immortal, bright!
Hearts moved, thus warmed, in union stir,
Responsive grow to things that were,
While man, our kindred through the past,
With us finds common goal at last.
Country! 'tis Heaven's great guerdon, boon,
Its rising star, a cloudless noon,
In its sweet sunshine pass away
The vaporing mists that round us lay;—
Touching the inmost sense and soul
With magic power, divine control;
Whate'er is great, and grand, and true,
It consecrates, gives charms anew,
All things sublimes, to Glory wed,
Its cloth of gold for man is spread;
He walks abroad with lordly gait,
No cringing thralls around him wait,
Magnanimous, heroic, brave,
Spurning abjectness, tyrant, slave,
Each valued gift he fond bestows,
In deep'ning stream his bounty flows,
Nor difference 'mong his equals knows.
The moral virtues, grand and rare,

True greatness, glory, made its care,
Baptisms giving wrongs surcease,
Grand pregnancies of 'during peace,—
Imperial thoughts of quick'ning fire,
Great deeds heroic, that inspire,
Structures the earthquake cannot rend,
Beauty, grandeur, that knit and blend,
Unveiling harmonies of light,
Secrets that yield pure, sweet delight,
Pouring Heaven's radiance bright, around,
Making all sacred, hallowed ground,—
Great citadel to shield the race,
Fortress where Right finds shelt'ring place,
Ends high and holy, proud its toil,
Through ages dimming tyrant spoil,—
Who can but venerate, esteem,
A power august, thus grand, supreme!
Whence come improvements, culture, taste?
Thrive they on Nature's unpruned waste?
Choice excellencies, glories rare,
The noblest virtues ages bear,
Devotion, patriotism, zeal,
Impulse the holiest man can feel,—
Can they be found unfenced where lie,

All things in rude barbarian dye?
Whence Time's great legacies of light,
That blaze with dazzling lusters bright,
Changing the human lot, estate,
Uplift, shape, mould, arts invocate,
That polish manners, grace, give ease,
Instruct, make wise, the virtuous please,
The brave, heroic, nerve, make strong,
To roll the centuries' hopes along,—
Whence dates their origin, their birth,
Making this brambled Eden earth?
'Tis Country's, civilization's voice,
Bids nations in their march rejoice;—
Whether Egyptian, Tyrian power,
Shrines, temples build, high wall and tower,
Or 'neath Time's star, some modern world,
New ensign, banner, hath unfurled,
'Tis the uplifted, pillar'd State,
Divorced from wrong, oppression's weight,
That puts on Power its starry crown,
Sends Time's great gifts the ages down!
Country! O, 'tis our nobler part,
Great, all-embracing, folding heart,
Guardian, bright shield, strong lover, loved,

Great Magnet, by which hearts are moved,
Deliverer, Guide, Attendant, Friend,
Glory's proud nurse, whose aims transcend!
When all in-breathed with radiant life,
Afar the storms of passion, strife,
When pure ambitions spotless shine,
Flash and thick ray with beams divine,
Its life-throbs pulse, give quickening thrill,
With pride, strong patriot bosoms fill,—
With grandeur, majesty, elate,
It flashes boundaries bright to Fate!
Our mother from whose breasts we draw
Protection, order, safety, law,
The life-blood whence our being thrives,
Whose nurturing stream Time, change sur-
    vives.
Untold its lovely, roseate charms,
When sympathy, devotion, warms,
With burning, grand, escutcheon'd zeal,
It stamps e'ermore the common weal;—
Fountain of valor, genius, power,
When omens threaten, dim the hour,
Prophetic of that earthquake tread
That dims Fate's star, or plumes its head,

Hurling dread thunderbolts through air,
Fearless to do, devise, and dare,
The great incorporate, quenchless Life
It breasts huge storms of battle strife,
Heaves granite mountains from their base,
Can piled up century wrongs erase,—
With giant tread can shake a world,
'Neath Freedom's starry flag unfurled,—
Doom policies of madness, wrath,
That darken Time's unlaurell'd path,
Upturn each stately monarch throne,
That dares man's rights contemn, disown,
With whirlwind, with tornado blast,
Turn ruin's myrmidons aghast,
That rush with violence supreme
On reason's lighting, warning beam;
Who dare th' eternal God defy,
Rout and consign to infamy!—
Its essence, Truth, pregnant with might,
Herculean can grasp and smite,
Bring proud oppressors towering down,
Kings, potentates, tyrants, uncrown;
Pretentious lords in wild dismay,
Scatter by one outflashing ray,

Immortal man unchained make free
To taste thy sweets, O, Liberty!
When streams of blood to bridles flow,
Earth one vast realm of nightshade, woe,
Where demon eyeballs glare and rage,
Man doomed dread war with hell to wage ;
When all Heaven's vials, uncorked, run
Wrath, terror, darkening stars and sun,
All fountains surging, foaming deep,
Black, roaring maelstroms dizzying sweep ;
Loud shrieks of agony, despair,
Loading th' encumbered, staggering air,
Creation wild with starless gloom,
Waiting the crash of red-lipped doom ;
Great patriots trembling as they cry
For innocence with tear-pearl'd eye ;
O, then 'mid onsets deepening far,
Rising its million'd-mirroring star,
Waving red flaming wings of war,
As in imperial glowing form,
It peers above the dreadful storm,
Loud thunders rolling murderous peal,—
Hope waiting on the deadly steel,
Fierce lightnings blazing down the sky,

Unblenched its eagle glancing eye;
'Neath waving crest of Glory bright,
It hurls the centuries' foes in flight;
Country! it stars the course of Time,
Towers a grand beacon flame sublime,
Lights the vast stage where nations play,
And empires bear the palms away,—
Where Destiny in fitful turn,
As fall the sands from Time's great urn,
Hurls dynasties, once sovereign, great,
The humble, small, to elevate,
New altars kindling for the truth,
Crowns Freedom with perennial youth;
Dependence, Friendship, light again,
Joy, peace succeed to sorrow, pain,
While sinks oppression's cruel reign!
Country indeed may be but name,
When Honor, Glory, sink in shame,—
When Freedom from her altar fires,
Spurned, vilified, from earth retires,
Coming instead relentless train,
Despotic with dark iron chain,
To bind and manacle man's soul,
Dim natal star, his final goal,

10

When infamy, when perjuring wrong,
O'erwhelm the weak, and crush the strong;
When sets the star of progress bright,
In desolation's hopeless night,—
Then, though heaven's sun may pour bright
    beams,
Leap, rush, melodious mountain streams,
Vales waft their odorous, sweet perfume,
Hills, mighty plains, bud, smile in bloom;
Country! 'tis but a living tomb,
Where man his manhood flung away,
His noble powers sink in decay;
Lingering 'mid monumented fame,
No deed of Glory stars his name;
The past all powerless, vision dim,
No inspiration hath for him;
Like some tall wreck hove on the shore,
That crumbles and is seen no more,
All, all unpitied in his woes,
He sinks unenvied to repose,
While Lethe's water dark o'erflows!
Let but the tide of fortune turn,
He chains, and fetters, valiant spurn,
Call on his country, 'mid his need,

To break his bonds, and he be freed;—
Lo! what expansion clothes him now,
With manhood's garland on his brow;
In unison with centuries strong,
Their diapason in his song;—
Country, redeemer, towering shines,
Around its brow he garland twines,
Bows at its shrine, lowly he kneels,
His patriot vows in meekness seals.
Invading foes may ravage, stride,
Spread devastations far and wide,
The mightiest monuments deface,
Symbols of glory mar, erase,
Dim its escutcheon flaming bright,
'Till sets its star 'mid deepening night,
'Till scarce a vestige trace is seen
Of ancient grandeur, Glory, mien;
Bright as the eternal arch of blue,
It lives embalmed in memory's view;
Ages may glide, the centuries roll,
From sire to son it fires each soul,—
Wins veneration, fond esteem,
From generations while they dream!
Country! O, 'tis a living power,

To quicken, vivify, endower,
To Chaos, Anarchy's wild reign
Brings back Law, Order, Peace, again;
Feuds, dire convulsions endless quells,
As freedom's healing current swells,—
Dooms usurpation, seals with woe,
Dark tyrannies gives overthrow,
Causing new streams of good to flow,
New fields to bud, new harvests grow!
Country! Sweet Home! ah, who can tell
The magic of their potent spell;
When envied by the strong, the proud,
Dark, fearful omens overcloud;
When deep disasters thick enshroud,
When Hope's sweet sunshine dims afar,
And night falls 'round its glittering star;
When fierce ambition, void of shame,
Bids plunder stalk, despoil their fame;
Peals then the tocsin blast of war,
Near, wide around, from realms afar,
Comes fearful struggle, shout, huzza,
Of mighty legions, gathering fast,
In valor, prowess unsurpassed,
Moving like whirlwind's fiery blast,

Th' invader down to ruin cast,—
Heroic forces:—read the Past,
As Time its fortunes hath re-cast!—
Of Greek, on that conspicuous day
When Persia's hosts fled in dismay,
When 'long Minerva's classic strand
Th' invading pirate hordes disband:
Of Roman, as with valor's might,
He clove in twain, put foes to flight.
Carrying his eagles around the world,
His flag by day, by night, unfurl'd!
Listen, hear Poland's piercing cry,
When fierce Hussar, Cossack, were nigh,
The rending of Italia's moan,
The Magyar's deep desponding groan,—
When freedom trampled long in dust,
Sharp glittering steel the patriot's trust!
Country! Sweet Home! all peerless, grand,
Eternal monuments they stand!
Bright flaming lode-stars, Glory-spanned,
Their talismanic memories start,
They rouse, they fire the patriot heart,
Nerve heroes in their champion fight,
To vindicate eternal Right;

To rout man's foes, put them to flight,
Preserve the treasures, sweet and dear,
The grandest blessings of the sphere;
Lead in each struggle's bloody van,
Home, Country, watchword, fellow-man,—
When soiled their banners, steeped in gore,
Able to stem the tide no more;
The noblest instincts warm the strife,
Where man for country yields his life!
That can imperial arts renew,
Trace Time's vast footprints centuries through.
Rare policies by statesmen build,
The common weal protect, enshield;
Open to Progress higher sphere,
From paths to glory rubbish clear,
Guide man's proud race to high renown,
With greatness, honor, glory, crown!
To such a power, transcendant, great,
Ne'er young, ne'er old, the ceaseless state,
Whose silver stream forever flows,
Though man may change, no respite knows,—
Their faith, devotion, substance, prayer,
The Pilgrims bring an offering rare;
There see the social virtues rise,

Life bloom in sweet, unsullied dyes,
When guardian of true liberty,
From pompous rites, pageants, set free,
Religion, with Heaven's blessing great,
Pours splendor, brightness round the State!
When civil structures, lifted, grand,
With moral virtues bright o'erspanned,
Life traced in every feature rare,
Of burdens, blessings, equal share,
Munificence, true taste displayed,
Genius, in noblest light arrayed,
Flashing its splendor-darting beam
Of truth, of justice, right, supreme,
Illumined mind, creative grown,
Quickened, starring new mental zone,
Bright constellations, grand to shine,
Galaxies from Heaven's golden mine,
Imperial, their brightening train,
Pledge, guardian of true Wisdom's reign,
Unrivaled skill, contrivance wise,
All in which greatness, grandeur, lies,
Unloosed, quickened, sweet fruits to yield,
True national glory thus revealed,
Towers monumental, grand, sublime,

Refulgent grows through deepening Time!
There, as the future ages see
How hero valor makes man free,
His sacrifice for liberty,
By what persistent, matchless force
Was shaped Time's checkered, dubious course,
How, 'mid conflicting passions, war,
Rolled on humanity's great car,
How Fortune, Fame,—how Glory sped,
How man from bondage lift his head,
New, living Power, bright'ning apace,
Freedom encrown a rising race,
Man's birthright walled with fire around,
Impregnable, a sacred ground,
That sacrilegious power that there
Attempts to desolate, make bare,
Waste, spoil, suborn, destroy that prize,
Condemned, in ignominy dies;—
Country in glory, not in shame,
Waxes, becomes earth's beaconing flame,
Where, 'neath religion,—faith, true zeal,
Time's grandest destinies fulfil!
Bearing to ages Heaven's great law,
The Pilgrims, led by pious awe,

Deep-moved, august, lo! they revere
The powers sublime, enthroning here;
Stately, illustrious, grand, quick grown,
Endowed with strength unmatched, unknown,
Structures rare, emblematic, true,
Wisdom resplendent, born anew,
To serve mankind, the ages through,
Meet human want, supply man's need,
From ancient follies, bondage, freed.
Constrained, impelled by Faith and Love,
Their mission sprung from Heaven above,
Rooted in God's eternal plan,
Deliverance bearing high to man,
Seeking vast boundaries for their reign,
Terrestrial empire here to gain,
New realms for Faith's supreme control,
New starting for an endless goal;—
When at Heaven's shrine they bow, confess,
Oft ask their Guardian God to bless
This land---washed by two oceans deep,
Whose waves, wild, musical, loud, sweep
In diapason evermore,
For Right and Union, thunder, roar.
Great land, to them but dimly known,

Gigantic now, collossal grown,
Where, 'neath Heaven's cope, wide overhead,
God's brightest constellations spread;—
Where mighty rivers, from the pole
To tropic gulfs their waters roll,
Where mountain heights in sunlight dressed
By guardian bands of Freedom pressed,
Thunder with dread, volcanic ire,
Spouting black, lava-flames of fire,
Or through eternal robes of snow,
In roseate hues of crimson glow,
Reflect Heaven's pure, sweet love on high,
In each exquisite, matchless dye,—
Lifting proud bulwarks to the sky,
Grand towers of watching Deity,
Far-ranging,—'neath which vallies spread,
Grand plains, where myriad freemen tread;—
Vast land of civil arts, true power,
With fame unstained, perennial flower,
A land, should tyrants 'tempt its life,
Heroes like stars would crown the strife
Millions of flashing sabers gleam,
Freedom's great ensigns wave and stream;—
To save from ruin's vortex wide,

Each patriot's burning, holiest, pride,
Whose flaming orb, quenched in 'mid sky,
Would fall Heaven's tear, and millions sigh!
Their trophy,—they the founders old,
Pilgrims immortal, Heaven-enrolled,
To faith, right, reason, love, true fear,
They give to build vast empire here,
Great home, where every charm refined,
Shall grace, adorn, build up mankind.
Patrons of all that finds true birth,
Home, country, beaconing lights of earth,
Guarding with jealous, loyal aim,
Far, far beyond Time's transient flame,
They glance their quickening, purging sight,
To realms invisible of light,—
Realms of unending, sweet repose,
Where decks Heaven's fadeless, blooming
     rose;—
'Neath Faith's bright banner, high unfurled,
Thither would guide mankind a world!
What mission, say, through Time so grand
As that the Pilgrims meekly planned,
Led through the deep, by Heaven's right hand,
To plant and build this mighty land?

Were they the men by power distressed,
By cruel tyrants torn, oppressed,
By prejudice, by cruel hate,
Flung from the social, civil State,
Mulcted, imprisoned, fettered, bound,
Hunted like beasts creation round!
While pampered luxury could feed,
Licentious, wanton, fill with greed
Of sordidness,—with groveling aims,
In riot kindling damning flames,
Create, fling round, dark mischiefs vile,
Ensnare the weak, the pure beguile,
Foul, vile ambition, in its chair,
Blessed by the pampered curate's prayer,
Heaven's truth eclipsed, with foul disdain,
All blackening vices called to reign,—
A court debauched, royalty doomed,
Transgression, crime, at mid-day plumed,
Dread parliament, purlieu of hell,
With gaps, dark fissures, demon spell,
Where hooting fiends, wild devils yell,
Fearful of Truth's most distant smell!
Fortune's, the favored sons of Time,
Fleeing all justice, 'spite their crime!

Were they the men must feel the rod,
Meek, chosen champions of their God?
Alas! with bigotry, false zeal,
They 're branded, pests fanatical,
Of too straight conscience, straighter life,
Hair-splitters, waking endless strife,
Demure in mein, with downcast face,
Turning mankind by sheer grimace,
Pretending that to be man's right,
Kings, princes, nobles, put to flight,
Contemn, deep scorn, with stubborn will,
The same thing tyrants doomed do still!
They were the men the powers that be
Clothed in the blackest infamy;—
Bowing in sorrow for God's church .
Grown lordly, they must feel the birch;
Asking for apostolic times,
They 're charged with diabolic crimes;
Faith once delivered to the saints
Besmirched with ochre, daubed with paints,
Conventicle for glass with stain
Chosen, no goodness can remain,—
Lo! godless clan, with zealot's brain,
Fittest for mad-house, maniac train,

With Satan leagued,—the cloven foot,—
All ranks may curse, o'erpower, uproot,
The State be summoned to the task,
No quarter given, though quarter asked,
Pursue as fire-brands, burn as straw,
Upheld by courts, tribunals, law ;—
Send into exile, banish far,
To pine 'neath pestilential star,
Where, like base culprits though they live,
They o'er their wicked course may grieve.
They were the men, slander thus vile
Heaped with its venomous, bitterest bile,
Named foul schismatics, baleful crew,
Damnation, blackest, hottest, due!
Dissenters, restless, unappeased,
With spiritual fancies sore diseased,
Fired by prude whims, capricious light,
In place of Duty, angel bright.
Slander! the foulest imp of hell,
Satan's companion when he fell,
Grown nothing pure from lapse of Time,
Drinking obliquities from crime,
Impelled by inward malice, rage,
War endless in its wrath to wage,

It brands them, innocent, with shame,
Foul blots, would endless mar their fame,—
But Time is wise,—they disenthral,
Their fetters, foul reproaches, fall ;
Towering o'er ages once supreme,
They give mankind a central beam,
Send new, great pulse-tides from their heart,—
Earth, Time, the Centuries, re-start,
With lightning shocks of living truth,
To run career of endless youth !
Smoothing the wrinkles of a world,
By error dim'd, midnighted, whirled,
Disjointed, riven, begloomed, distressed,
Cajoled, o'er-tyrannized, oppressed,
Sweet concords, harmonies, they find,
In heavenlier ties the earth they bind,
Give smiles,—forelight with noble joy,
Existence purge of base alloy.
They were the men, when Time was new,
Flung shadow from the Image true,
Aye, rayed Heaven's pure, immortal light,
Dropt splendors on the gloom of night ;—
God's hero-souls of living fire,
Whom undertakings vast inspire,

Sublimities beyond the sky,
Magnificences, grandeurs high,
Glories endless, firing their eye,
Unborn realities they try,—
Dangers, dark perils, death, defy,
To reach grand goal for which they sigh.
Of forecast, shrewdness, subtle, strong,
Rolling Time's mightiest powers along,
Down-shut the world to feeble sense,
Kindling with longings deep, intense,
For Beauty's realm, spiritual, severe,
Soaring, Faith points God's endless year,
Poising, they there in light, insphere,
In meditations joyful, dear,
Visions of glory brighten clear,
Lo! things impalpable come near,
Th' Unseen, unfolding, they revere,
Sweet, high revealments Heaven endear,
Celestial brightness conquering fear,—
Vast Mount of Being! blazing high,
Peers on their rapt, entranced eye,
Foundations massive, starry, high,
Of sapphire, emerald, pearly dye,
Far-towering heights, in glory spanned,

Far-opening vistas, beauteous, grand,

Paths Heaven's eternal wisdom planned,

Far, far beyond Time's wreck-strown strand,

Perfection's home, its Beulah land,

Welcome to earth's worn Pilgrim band!

There, forms of excellence supreme

Dart Beauty's warmest, brightest beam,

Each point of space a sparkling gem,

Emblazoning scepter, diadem!

Rank peering rank, o'ertopping, deep,

In serried grandeur, station keep,

Disorder, discord, all unknown,

In that sublime, seraphic zone!

There light's sweet, softest, billows pour,

There fan sweet gales, that sweep Heaven
    o'er,

Eternal day, no darksome night,

God's myriad hosts, fair, spotless, white,

Immortal, radiant, dazzling throngs,

Pouring sweet hallelujah-songs,

Charming each ravished, list'ning ear,

Which heard in Time, would all unsphere!

By faith, that Mount they buoyant climb,

Scale the tall summits, grand, sublime,

'Mid brightening walks, fair flowers in bloom,
Sharon's sweet rose, lily's perfume,
Sparkling acclivities outrise,
Fair landscapes, greeting blissful eyes,
Far-spreading scenes of wondrous joy,
Myriads at heavenly tasks employ,
Sweet, fanning zephyrs, dropping balm,
All grateful stirred, th' eternal calm;—
Upward they mount, cease not to rise,
Heaven turning on them all its eyes,
With Love's sweet notes of sacrifice,
Ethereal growing, unsurpassed,
New wonders breaking on them fast,
Transfiguring glories, nearing, far,
The soul of song through all the air,
Till 'mid the central mount supreme,
Beauty enthroned with purging beam,
There, in the living, quenchless rays,
The flaming summit all ablaze,
They bow;—'tis Heaven's high, holy shrine,
Where roll sweet splendors pure, divine,
Where fragrance falls, where souls inspire,
Enkindle with immortal fire,
Find knowledge endless, e'er to grow,

Increase, augment, all bounds o'erflow,
Truth, justice, love, unchanging right,
Starred with celestial features bright,
Undimmed by mortal error's night !
Great principles for every land,
Relations social, moral, grand,
God, God Himself hath wisely planned,
Espoused, applied, in practice true,
Would earth to paradise renew.
Purging their vision in that light,
Transfiguring in sweet radiance bright,
They feel them near that spotless throne,
Where wrong, injustice, ne'er were known,
See starred, bright, new-robed Destiny
Put on its crown, fair Liberty !—
Pilgrims, they through their being feel
Heaven's approbation blissful steal,
With fond delight, enravished glow,
Conquer, o'ercome their pain and woe.
There, 'mid the radiance deep. they find
Great lessons they would teach mankind,
Lessons of wisdom, life, and peace,
Whose quick'ning power shall never cease.
Steadfast, long gazing, as they turn,

Love's quenchless fires deep kindle, burn,
They muse on homes, the loved away,
Within dim gates of mortal day,
Of sorrows, fears, that there control,
While waves of Light break o'er their soul,
Prelude the peaceful, nearing rest,
In the high kingdoms of the blest,
Taste that sweet joy that knows no end,
When earthward swift their footsteps tend!
Laden with treasures of the skies,
Truth's glowing immortalities,
Lo! they descend, to Earth return,
Satanic kingdoms, empires, spurn,
Light altars new, to brightly burn,
No toilsome task for man adjourn,
No arduous duty, work, postpone,
The Present seize, Future unknown,
Kindling with Glory's waking power,
They beacon that fast coming hour
When God's great cycles shall fulfil,
Revered His word, obeyed His will,
When all shall own, confess His name,
Nor deem His service drudgery, shame!
Christ's living church, a spotless bride,

Its growth, perfection, e'er their pride,
For that they sacrifice, they pray,
Nor cast their confidence away.
Stone from the mountain, glorious, grand,
To wax, increase, fill every land,
'Mid wrath, disaster, oft defeat,
Its foes o'erpowered, in swift retreat,
Of humble aspect, pompless, pure,
Its triumph certain, victory sure,
Like them the Pilgrims, all unknown,
Through wilderness, to struggle, groan,
Its paths by fiery pillar shown,
Nations subduing, mighty grown,
Through deep'ning light, a bright'ning zone,—
To pass, all-radiant, to Heaven's throne,
In blissful service, songs, sweet praise,
Crowned with immortal, endless days.
Christ's church, its living, spotless fame
Dearer than life, than world-prized name,
Rescued, confessed, maintained its claim,
Which hypocrites dare not defame;
Home, Country, lit by Freedom's flame,
Guarded by power unselfish, wise,
Their patterns dropt from out the skies;

Based on God's Truth, eternal Right,
Suffused all radiant with Heaven's Light,
Their perilous mission they complete,
Then bow before the mercy seat!
Lost millions point to Jesus' feet,
Each prodigal returning greet;
Seek for new world, virtue's career,
Light that shall burn through every sphere,
Earth of its dross, its rubbish clear;
Blessings supreme, Heaven's watching eye
To guard, defend, when dangers nigh.
Were they from Heaven's eternal Light,
Transfiguring 'mid its radiance bright,
Pilgrims of day, dreading foul night,
Th' eternal God their Rock, Delight,
Confessed, acknowledged by his might!—
Were they the men for Folly's scowl,
For Atheism's vulgar howl,
Besotted libertine's dark jeer,
Base infidel's defaming sneer?—
Who with proud upward longings high,
By Faith beyond the starry sky,
Scale Glory's apex, from Heaven's day,
Pour sweet refulgence on man's way,

Make Truth and Right, on earth supreme,
Time ray with Heaven's eternal beam,
Freedom's great Light pass swift abroad,
Hastening the triumphs of their God!
Men 'mid these wondrous modern times,
Whose grandeur distance now sublimes,
Majestic, towering, at whose tread,
Earth tremble on her granite bed!
As clouds of prejudice, of scorn,
Dissolve, 'mid blush of mightier morn,
Seen mightiest names of flesh e'er born,—
Great herald guides, God sent the race
Truth to uphold, error displace,
To point the goal of true desire,
Kindle a grand, unwaning fire;
Then through Time's laurel'd arch supreme,
Retire, flash brightening, living beam,
Quenchless from out the mighty Past,
In Glory, Power, Light, unsurpassed!—
Men of a brightening, radiant mould,
Stern, unseduced by lucre gold,
Starring new age of heraldries,
Of undertakings, enteprise,
Of movements mighty, well begun,

Achieving victories, triumphs won,
Germ seeds, for future ages grand,
To burst in fruitage o'er each land.
Are they the men to disesteem,
To brand fanatical, extreme?
Men of illustrious pedigree,
Great Freedom's consanguinity,
Bearing bright mace of generous power,
Just, equal rights, Time's grandest dower,—
Hailed the great almoners of God,
Diffusing righteousness abroad;
Of burning, never-quenching zeal,
Whose noble souls could deeply feel
For all the woes of human kind,—
The mightiest burdens, loose unbind,—
Color, complexion, nation, clime,
No bar to Heaven's gifts sublime;
Life's message bearing true to all,
The humble, wise, the great, the small;
Joyed like one grander in his day,
To rend all obstacles away;
Break the huge brazen barriers strong,
Walling the ages, dark and long;
Give human nature grandest way

In Life's vast tragic drama-play.
While others stint their generous aim,
And for themselves compassions claim,
The crystal streams they open wide,
With their own selfishness deep dyed,
All generous plans, great systems wise,
Chosen for fame in human eyes,
They disinterested, doomed to rise,
Born for the noblest sacrifice,
Content, should they forgotten be,
In exile and obscurity,
To live, toil, labor, die unknown,
Their God to Honor, Truth enthrone,
A world enfranchise, man make free,
A Future glorious yet to see!
Men of magnanimous, great soul,
Of deep devotion, high control,
Whom ages wrapt in homage sweet,
With rising millions, haste to greet!
Men who could lay hands on the flood,
Sweeping sublime, the march of God,
On crested mountain billows steep,
Amid their roar find balmy sleep,
Dark, cresting Ocean's wrath defied,

Its torrents stem with hero pride;
New Hemispheres give human eye
To brighten, while the centuries fly ;
Their mountain pinnacles sublime,
Vast, roseate peaks, thresholds of Time,
To fairer lands. Heaven's sweet repose,
Where endless, blooms its fragrant rose,
Where beauty, change, nor dimness knows,
Where river of life forever flows !
Men who, ordained ages to free,
Sounded all depths of Truth's great sea,
Passed jagged gorges, lit with fire,
By its Eternal Author, Sire,
Abysms matchless, mighty, spanned,
Huge labyrinths, their windings grand,
Vast heights ascended, soaring far,
'Neath Time's all-radiant, dazzling star,
Beyond all worlds, that mystic lie
In starry depths of azure sky,
The Good, the True, the Fair, to find,
Vast legacies for all mankind,
Of glory, grandeur, priceless worth,
Since Time's beginning without birth;
Who mightiest problems scanned, profound,

Flung sunlight world-wide, nations round,
Gave all things quickening, mightier bound;
Still seeking high, still higher ground,
Soar far beyond Time's twilight sun,
Scan the immortal races run,
See where great destinies are spun,
Wove in pure beams of Heaven's white throne,
'Mid splendor's radiant, burning zone,
See flashing domes, far gleaming spires,
Heaven's matchless, flaming altar fires,
Hear the deep thunder of that song,
In diapasons thrilling, strong,
Rolling Heaven's airs sublime along,
Rapt utterance of immortal tongue!
Are they the men for beardless fools
To mock, despise, with ruffian tools
For slander's poison-pointed dart
To pierce with pangs, till life-blood start,
For faithless men to implicate,
Brand infamous in Church and State?
Alas! degenerate are the days,
Man turns to Folly's wicked ways,
For ancient faith the fathers taught,
Concupiscence and lust are wrought,

By groveling passions of the world,
From Glory's summit man is hurled,
To wander, darkling, vulgar stray,
Farther, still farther from right way;
Though kindled by ethereal fire,
He sinks, o'erwhelmed, in deepest mire,
Blasting his hope, his reason dark,
Quenching proud being's deathless spark!
But I, no prophet, yet will tell
That ancient faith shall with us dwell.
There is, in human conscience deep,
An ocean, where the gales that sweep
Drive Heaven-ward for true spiritual rest,—
Prenatural sense, in whose strong quest
For peace, pure light from kingdoms blest,
Reflected dim, Heaven is possessed!
Earth, it is wayward; Time is drear;
A Godless mind hath bondage, fear;—
Men cannot yet uproot themselves,
Grow irresponsible, turn elves,
Fairies, as evanescence light,
Dancing on moonbeams of the night.
Mind, 'tis a nobler, kinglier stock,
Must build on Heaven's Eternal Rock,

Else dire convulsions, earthquakes shock,
Satanic foes assail and mock.
Gazing on Nature, all can feel
Her beauteous forms, awake their zeal,
Her gorgeous suns, fair moons, bright stars,
Her mingling clouds, sweet draperies,
Effulgence bursting through a world
In roseate dyes of crimson, gold,
Robes, robes of purple, scarlet, fire,
Whose trailing glories gods inspire,
Swept thro' the vaulted arch, Heaven's dome,
By angel bands from out their home;
Sent on some mission heavenly, grand,
To deck, adorn earth's lovely land,
With what enrapturing, sweet delight
They ravish, charm our mortal sight;
A world pavilion'd, flaming bright
In glory, day heralding night,
All august scenes, magnificence,
Her pomps of power, omnipotence,
The tempests march, the torrents plunge,
Th' imprison'd air's earthquake revenge,
The crash, the boom, of wilderness,
The falling tree, its loneliness,

The flashing pool, mirror of God,
Sweet daisy, flow'rets on the sod,
The ever changing, varying dyes,
Aspects, fair features, that surprise,
They make her realm vast palace fair,
Man's joyous pastime oft to share!
Scanning high art, that, too, inspires,
Stirs inward, deep, Promethean fires;
Beneath cathedral, temple, arch,
Columns where centuries hold their march,
Lo! how vast, mighty spirits thrill,
As virtues from the Past distil;—
As bursts the cloud, its radiant star,
With smile of Glory beaming far,
Hope-light of Future, mightier, grand,
Great guerdon of each unblessed land.
Transfiguring Life, lo! silent, speaks,
Th' eternal doom of slumber breaks,
When Art the ages re-awakes,
Then man, oblivion dark forsakes,
Life's blushing beauty, grace returns,
In fond presentment glowing, burns!
But who, his inmost nature known,
To whom Time's wonders have been shown,

Coupled with outward, earthward sight,
Hath hungered not for spiritual light!
Sense, it is shallow,—grandest pile,
Bright hues, fair colors, may beguile,
Mind's deeper wants can ne'er repair,
To spiritual voidance, mist and air.
Not isolate, struck from the throne
Is man,—but to his Maker known.
Vast system folds him, right or wrong,
Resistless currents bear along;
'Mid powers unseen, vast forces grand,
His destiny eternal, planned,—
He drinks in influence, takes in food,
Th' spiritual, Fair, Beautiful, Good,
Quenching his thirst, his hunger o'er,
As light breaks from the eternal shore.
All feel that Faith is needed here,
Its light gone out, what else can cheer?
Can markets, gewgaws, boisterous wealth,
Futurity in muffled stealth,
Close at each heel, to whirl away,
The butterflies that last a day?
I do not envy such as these,
The sons of Folly, ill at ease,

Impelled by sense of sight, of sound,
Scourged, lashed, self-gauntleted around,
Loaded with chains, passions impose,
To which are light all common woes.
Lo! giddy France, where is she now,
Blasphemer who refused to bow,
Dark skeptic of the modern school,
Who 'mid Faith's wonders played the fool!
Nations as man, must have firm root,
Else Heaven will trample under foot;—
In paths of truth ordained to go,
Facing all hostile winds that blow,
No idiosyncracies refined
Can purge the vision of the blind,
Allure the erring, point the way
To light and sunshine, heavenly day.
Walking deep, sightless paths of Time,
Where lurk temptation, envy, crime,
Where every doubtful, devious road
Leads from the true, the only Good;
Where nature's intuitions wise,
To grasp, decide, ne'er, ne'er suffice;
Pregnant, but not with spiritual right,
To choose the only course of Right,

Where earth-born passions aims control,
Deepening the darkness of each soul,
Whelming in sloughs of endless mire,
Where being's embers, quenched, expire;
No innate, inwrought, quickening beam,
No balance, guidance-power supreme,
To thread the awful mazes deep,
Guide where the head-long torrents sweep;
No sweet Elysian, heaven-born strain
To lull the heart's deep, saddening pain;
Tossed, tempest-beat, on Life's dark main,
What but some high, supernal force
Can steady human nature's course,
Touching deep springs, all, all unseen,
Life's perils, dangers, stand between;
Lift sovereign wand, a power divine,
At which eternal light shall shine,
Calm all disturbance, lust, and rage,
Heaven for weak man its strength engage!
Faith, mighty Faith, 'twas Heaven-ordained,
Earth's mightiest sons, prophets, sustained,
Linked by its power to Heaven's high throne,
Chosen, in God's high purpose known,
Purchased by Him who came to atone,

14

From Heaven and who himself once gave
A rebel world, redeemed, to save;
Such, such the fall, alone outrise,
Beacon the earth, and gain the skies,
Spread Christ's salvation without bound,
Wake songs the universe around.
Joined with sweet Hope, fair charity,
The bright, immortal sisters three,
Whose several fires united burn,
Man hero lives, earth's gods can spurn;
Achieve great deeds, endless to shine,
Fair, fairest garland-wreaths entwine,
Immortal honors win divine.
Would man be strong, invincible?
Faith, that must be his principle.
Craves he the boon of rare success?
Wearing Faith's shield, God then can bless.
No righteous boon will He withhold
From those within its mystic fold.
Immortal faith, hope, charity,
A three-fold cord, great mystery,
With anchor in the rock cleft thrown,
The human bark by hurricane's blown,
Maintains its poise, a wreck ne'er known;

Through fiery tempests called to sail,
Helm'd, rudder'd, compass'd, shall prevail;
Deeper than Time, broader than earth,
A power of high celestial birth
Presides, o'errules, directs the way;
Though hostile elements wild play
Around, their rage, their noise confound,
They fall, they perish at man's feet,
His victories, triumphs, ne'er defeat.
Who ride the tempest's furious blast,
When darkness, gloom all overcast,
When storms of vengeance gather deep,
And startling tempests onward sweep,
When mountain billows pile and roll,
And terror sinks each unarmed soul?
Those led by Heaven's eternal Star,
While 'round convulsions heave and war;
Nature in darkness deep, profound,
A radiance bright is flung around;
Like Israel, 'mid Egypt's night,
In Goshen cheered by Heavenly light!
See mighty martyr's stem the tide,
To Heaven on fiery chariots ride;
The reckless madmen who assail,

Quivering like ghosts as bloodless, pale,—
E'en woman, feeble child, at stake,
Lo! they death's awful terrors break;
Life's dreadful pangs swift flying past,
Eternal morning breaking fast!
Sustained by Faith, Hope's anchor strong,
They triumph over fear and wrong:—
God ne'er forsakes his loved, distressed,
'Mid tortures, agonies, gives rest.
See patriot virtues bright, supreme,
Man ground to dust, millstones between;
Thick darkness palling deep around,
See Bruce, a Wallace, strow the ground
With gnashing victims, heaps of slain,
Break the fierce tyrant's galling chain,
Point the bright path to Freedom's reign!
Lo! Tell's brave deed, on Alpine plain,
It sends through ages sweet refrain,
Immortalizing hero bands,
Starring with crowns great victor lands,—
Brighter than all the fame of kings,
Deliverance, glory, triumph brings,
From ignominies, bondage, shame,
Lighting with Heaven's eternal flame!

'Tis on the world's great days of power,
When direful storms tempestuous lower,—
When from oblivion's starless grave,
Man human heritage would save;
When thundering legions bristle, stare,
Hurl deadly bolts through darkening air,
Summoning resistance from despair,
Fearless to do, to brave and dare,
Rush in fierce onslaught,—Faith gives light,
Enstars the gloom of heaviest night
With glimpsing splendors, radiance bright,
Nerves each proud arm, each bosom fires,
Weakness with courage, strength, inspires,
The wavering, trembling, fills with zeal,
Makes heroes 'mid the loudening peal
Of deadly cannon, trumpet blast,
In valor, courage, unsurpassed!
When blood-red meteors wild fierce sweep,
And thousands fall in death's long sleep,
Death, carnage, seizing on their prey,
The thinning ranks filled with dismay,
Faith, Faith unmoved, leads on the van,
Yields not the cause of fellow man;
Peals the loud onset's clarion sound,

The field of strife makes hallowed ground!
Lo! where dark Danube's waters flow,
'Twas on that morn of human woe,
When gleamed fierce Tartar scimetar,
When Moslem waved his crescent dear,
When blood-stained hordes of savage men,
With horrid arms paled Europe's sun
With Asian vengeance, Asian crime,
Bent on the damning deed of Time,
To crush fair Truth 'neath mountain wave
Of warring men, dig its deep grave,
Scout Love, Redemption, from the world,
'Neath hell's black flag, in wrath unfurled!
Lo! as the awful summons came,
Faith, firm resolved, from Heaven aflame,
Leads each strong spirit up the height
In Europe's hour of bloodiest fight
For Truth, man's God-given birthright,
Exultant, trustful, undismayed,
There on high ramparts fierce arrayed,
Where foemen drew their glittering blade,
Where force 'gainst force in battle swayed,
Faith, unappaled, stems the dark tide,
Invincible though long defied,

Portcullis'd, marshall'd, at Heaven's side,
It pours the awful ruin wide,—
Turns back the lance, the flaming spear,
Of plumed, of glittering cavalier,—
Breaks serried ranks that fly and reel
Before the dreadful flaming steel ;—
Proud Turk, fierce Tartar, bite the dust,
Ambition drunk with battle thirst,
Fainting, o'erwhelmed, dismayed, distressed,
Th' unequal contest unconfessed !
Heaven's veiling sun in blood goes down,
Darkness vast, deep, the warriors drown ;
No living form through sunless air,
While blood and murder triumph there !
O, dismal scene of butchery, crime,
Hid from the sight of startled Time,
Dread scene of living horrors, death,
Of agonies, of fainting breath,
Of imprecations, curse and prayer,
Where hostile men their vows declare
'Mid wildest rage, lost hope, despair ;—
See Faith heroic, struggle, dare,
Send up to Heaven its pleading care,
Invoke for heroes Glory's share,

Victory or death ! its triumph there !
Fierce, fierce the onset, bloodier grows
The midnight carnage, slaughtering woes;
The light returns enwrapt in clouds,
The battling hosts thick gloom enshrouds;
Wild vengeance startles with a cry,
Red meteors flash along the sky,—
In vain;—Heaven breaks the blood-dyed
    scene,
The frowning ranks walks high between,
The startled hosts to madness driven,
Blow swift on blow, swift, dreadful, given,
Soon, soon the ramparts yield away,
And breaks glad morn of Europe's day!
Vast day of power, of glory, fame,
Of grand, immortal, heroes' name,
Of man's advancement, onward stride,
To high dominion, empire wide;
Builder of ages, in his pride,
The Past, the Future's, Teacher, Guide!
But strange, amazing, awful, vast,
The dyes that civilizations cast;
Influences shaping strong a world
By conflict, revolutions, hurled:—

One moment light, then darkness deep,
Brief calm, short peace, then billows steep
Hang their foam-crests amid the clouds,
While Hope's sweet star in gloom enshrouds!
Again o'ercast by treacherous guile,
By foul ambition's restless wile,
Debasing tyrants, despot clan,
Warring 'gainst God, 'gainst fellow-man,
Darkness returns, Egyptian night
Once more eclipses sovereign Right!
Not threatening curse of martial force,
Blockading ages in their course,
Dread, glittering arms, bright armor, steel,
Bristling in vengeance, Fate to seal;
Not savage legions, poured afar,
'Neath war's malignant, fiery star,
Rolling resistless in their pride,
With Desolation at their side,
Summon proud man, a world again,
To rise, with courage, might and main,
Hurl back th' invader, quench his flame
Of mad ambition, headlong, tame!
A foe more direful, sovereign, strong,
Intrenched for ages dark and long,

In human hearts, through hope and fear,
More dreadful than the glittering spear
Or bending lance the warrior breaks,
When conquering foe his path o'ertakes!
Invisible, dark, ghostly reign
Of priest-craft, with its spiritual chain
Of bondage, to which, common weight
Of tyrant wrong is light estate;
Darkening, its viewless cords to bind,
Shutting sweet knowledge from the mind,
By Jesuit craft, dark, subtle scheme,
Vile domination, foul, supreme,
It lifts its standards, awes a world,
With horrid ensigns wide unfurled;—
By dogmas, by traditions new,
By sophistries of hellish hue,
By rites, by fantasies untrue,
Authorities devoid of claim,
By villainies without a name,
Tricks, stratagems, of pagan shame,
It lures Heaven's flock within false fold,
Peeled, bartered, for vile pottage sold!
Unholy power, with pious awe,
Base superstition giving law,

Forcing submission, binding creed,
By torture, dungeon, bloodiest deed,
Inquisitorial purging fires!
O, Muse, say, did Hell's damning lyres,
Make music! they should give a sound
Chilling man's blood, freezing the ground,
Tell the sad, lonesome, horrid tale,
Of national bondage, barter, sale,
Of man oppressed, relentless torn,
Of every Heaven-lent lineament shorn,
Made thrall, vile serf, a beast of prey,
Prerogatives, rights, swept away,
'Neath priestly, crushing, tyrant sway,
Of Anti-Christ,—prophets foretold,
Piercing Time's haze from days of old ;—
In stolen robes of sacred light,
Filling a world with groans, affright,
More pagan than dark pagan night!
Foul monster, an embodied crime,
Concentered filth, pollution, slime,
Condensed depravity, vile scum,
Of arbitrariness, sin's sum,
Abominable infamies,
Of frauds, deceits, of deadly lies,

Trampling the earth 'neath blood-stained feet,
Thrusting itself in God's own seat,
To wreck its vengeance, crimes complete,
With lust of power ;—like Ætna's womb,
Where pent up fires e'er waste, consume!
Its summit throned where vapors lay,
Whose wreathing folds foretell dismay,
Whose awful sides when fierce they quake,
The mightiest thrones of monarchs shake,—
At whose dread, rumbling, earthquake sound,
Myriads turn ghastly pale, around,—
Whose lava-streams, shot fierce on high,
With scorching terrors tear the sky,
With dismal rage, projectiles flung,
With scornful hisses, fiendlike sprung,
Sent from hot Hell's consuming urn,
A world to deluge, blacken, burn,—
Sparing no beauteous, lovely thing,
No work of peasant, lord, or king,
With blighting, with devouring wrath,
Blasting all verdure in their path,
To barrenness, a lonely wild,
Turn nature, where an Eden smiled!
Thus dreadful the dread, priestly reign

Of tyrants, binding spiritual chain,
Bowing the soaring Godlike mind,
Clipping its wings to earth confined,
By fettering clogs, false, dismal glare,
Pomps, pageants, kept from native air,—
Sending forebodings, horror, fear,
Consumption through each wasting sphere,
Corruptions, iniquitous shame,
Profanities, without a name,
Hypocrasies, jugglings, deceit,
Libidinous, foul, lustful heat,
Lighted from Hell, on Earth re-born,
Virtue, sweet Innocence forlorn!
Th' Apocalyptic Anti-Christ,
With Earth's deep vileness subsidized,
The seven-hilled Beast lifted its head,
Ætnà-like, with vile harlots fed!
Poured, blasting, from its horrid mouth,
Eternal barrenness and drouth,—
Lighting the fagot, blazing torch,
Steeped in foul calumnies, debauch,
Hurling proud monarchs from their thrones,
A simoon, blighting through all zones,
By dread anathema's foul curse,

Too horrid for a sober verse!
Drunk with the blood of millions slain,
Palming indulgencies for gain,
Binding the earth with endless chain
Of vile abominations dark,
Trampled, extinguished, Freedom's spark.
All mighty landmarks of renown,
In one vast maelstrom swallowed down,
Earth swept by deluge, blasting fire,
Leaving no flower, no verdurous spire,
Far, far and near, deep, sullen gloom,
The living world, like death, a tomb!
Pealed then loud call of injured Time,
Faith, mighty Faith, dares deeds sublime,
Acts high transcendent, hero part,
Bids the pent world, renewed, re-start,
From the dead-rot of tyrant rule,
Taught from the skies in wisdom's school!
Gleams not proud crescent, scimetar,
Heard is no multitudinous stir
Of vengeful warriors, heated, rife,
To plunge in martial conflict, strife,
Roll the vast world in crimson flood
Of carnage, stain, with curse of God!

A single form, lo! walks Time's sea
Of blood, majestic, man to free!
With hand uplifted to the sky,
Waving Truth's banner proud on high,
A sacred halo breaking far,
Rising a new, unsetting star,
Portents, sweet omens, in their play,
Prognostic of a brighter day;
The nations waiting on each shore,
Watching forelightings gone before,
Who as they bow, high Heaven adore,
Deliverances unseen implore,—
Deliverances from error's curse,
From tyrant bondage, deep distress,
From ignorance, its deepening shame,
Relieved by Truth's outbursting flame!
In that vast crisis, lifted high,
God sends deliverance from the sky,
Beholds the hour, hears Faith's strong cry,
Breaks adamant, lone mountains dry
Bids send their streams, Faith's need supply,—
Provides his servant as of old,
In weakness, singleness, makes bold!
Grappling the dragon, scarlet whore,

See Luther light on darkness pour,
Dissolve th' enfolding clouds that lie,
Enwrap the world's great infamy,
Its starred abomination, vile,
Of lust, oppression, falsehood, guile!
Meek, mighty champion of his God,
He breaks the triple tyrants' rod,
Scorning prerogatives of air,
Pretentious claims, that never were
Of Heaven ordained for human use,
Vile usurpations, long abuse,
Of Heaven's mercy shown to man,
To light, not darken, his brief span,
Of being, on Time's perilous way
To reach the gates of endless day;
A bold reformer, spiritual knight,
Armored in Truth, celestial, bright,
He wields its lance, its glittering spear,
Hurls thunderbolts, Time's path to clear
Of spawning tyrants, priestly clan,
Robbers of God, immortal man,—
Through Faith bruises the bulwarks strong
Of sacrilegious error, wrong;—
Girded with might, in Heaven's high name,

He kindles Truth's eternal flame,
Beats back the swelling tides of power
That darken earth, mankind devour;
Makes monarchs quail before his tread,
Insulting princes bow their head,
Dread hierarchy, tossed and flung,
That human sighs and groans had wrung,
Through centuries, of hot despair,
Abomination, high in air!
Blasted its hope, with living ray,
Shot from the throne of endless day,
O'er Time's vast gloom sent radiance far,
As rose and blazed his hero star;—
Proud pope, vile ecclesiastic crew,
Priest, prelate, cardinal, o'erthrew,
Brings back the nation's hideous swung,
In blackening air,—where death knells wrung,
The pangs of martyrdoms, of woe,
Of vassalage,—from world laid low,
In abjectness,—rends the dark veil
Of guilt and horror that prevail,
Of vile debasements, errors strong,
Of infamies, of perjuring wrong;—
Europe, the nations, in its womb,
16

Summons to rise, burst from its tomb,
A world in darkness, night, gone down,
To rouse, run race of high renown,
For Truth, high Heaven's unfading crown!
Lo! at His voice the nations wake,
From sleep of ages sudden break,
Progress, its opened path they take,
False mum'ries, shibboleths forsake,
Hail the new light, serene and fair,
For Freedom, Truth, their God, declare!
By Faith's Herculean blow and bound,
Great Papacy struck to the ground,
Lo! bleeding victim, helpless, weak,
Powerless its vengeance more to wreak,
Blight the proud earth with error's curse,
Smit from its throne, stung with remorse ;—
Boasting false pedigree of power,
From Christ, the great apostle's hour,
Forever wounded, bruised its pride,
Ages shall curse, nations deride
As infamous, in robes of blood,
The dreadest scourge Time's path hath trod!
While he who dared to draw his bow,
And laid the triple monster low,

His friend, Phillippus Melancthon,
Great Fredericus, bold, brave Saxon,
They, who that great reform sped on,
Through God, the Father, Spirit, Son,
Immaculate Three, Heaven's Triune One,
As through long centuries, Truth shall shine,
Shall fresh, unfading garlands twine;
No period tire of their proud fame,
To speak the great reformer's name,
Luther's, a name deep, long embalmed,
Who rode the storm, the ages calmed,
Who to man's rights, to Freedom true,
'Gainst his vile foe dread missile threw,
Like Israel's monarch, with his sling
Who slew Philistia's giant king,
Raised up by Heaven, deliverer grand,
When darkness palled, struck dumb each land,
The waves fierce roaring, monarchs pale,
No arm of courage to prevail,
God's servant, nerved with hero might,
For Truth, eternal Justice, Right,
An humble monk, from out his cell,
By Faith, he routs the hosts of Hell,
Restores Truth's broken reign on earth,

Crowns civilization with new birth!
'Twas that same Faith made Pilgrims strong,
Eternal foes of error, wrong.
They caught that beam that blazed afar
From Germany's heroic star,
'Mid Alpine summits, throned on high,
Saw Zwingle, hero, martyr, die;
From Calvin, caught th' immortal fire,
God's chosen band, ages inspire;
But most from Christ, His living law,
The gospel, they their maxims draw.
Great-born of Time, they who had dared
Great deeds sublime, who bosoms bared
To Envy's shafts, malice, proud scorn,
That man might rise, earth be re-born!
They their examples, patterns bright,
'Mid their long, lone, dim, starless night,
Aiding, inspiring on their way,
To wide unbar new gates of Day.
In noble veins flows hero blood,
Since Adam, the engulphing flood,
In one vast bond, immortal tie,
Are linked great guides of Destiny,
Those who, by God's ordaining power,

Snap galling chains, re-'lume Time's hour,
With holier, new, shaping beam,
Make Right, Truth, Justice, Faith, Supreme!
Of that immortal, glorious band,
That thro' vast centuries toiled and planned
For human nature, Truth and Right,
The Pilgrims shine in deepening light.
The twisted cords of tyrant wrath,
Lo! they unbraid, fling from the path
Where true advancement flies apace,
Exalts, refines, the human race;
Soon, soon to light Time's farthest shore,
Dot with rare charms creation o'er,
Tame the rude savage in his wild,
Nature's untutored orphan child
Barbarian, 'mid her forest aisles,
Whom her rude sport, the chase, beguiles,
With more than Orphean soothing strain,
Hold earth in list'ning rapture's chain,
While Mercy, Love, in triumph reign!
O, wondrous change! 'tis Faith that brings
Deliverance to all human things,
As its pure, sparkling, crystal tide
Rolls through the kingdoms, empires wide,

See pomps, vile pageants, pass away,
Truth,. Reason, Right, begin their sway ;—
Dread superstitions lose their force,
New laws, new customs, change Time's course,
Just policies, arrangements wise,
Start tears of joy in human eyes,
New institutions, sagely planned,
Fling splendors o'er each burdened land;
Art, science, culture, root and grow,
Pure streams of nectar bounteous flow.
Deep, deep within immortal mind,
Comes consciousness to Heaven resigned,
A holy trust, pure, rich and sweet,
High hopes of happiness complete!
Some bow of sorrow may be sprung,
Some silent grief may find a tongue,
Some disappointment sudden rise,
Deep anguish moisten tearless eyes,
Misfortune, calumny, fierce hate,
Friendship's fond smiles, its love abate,
Mankind may frown, mock, disesteem,
Drawn tyrant-swords flash, blood-red gleam,
Rack, torture, dungeons, noisome, dark,
May quench life's momentary spark,

The sun eclipse, come terrors, night;
Nature's sweet charms all wither, blight,
Dark tempests pile, huge billows sweep,
Volcanic fires in madness leap,
Dark demons spit their malice, ire,
The devils burst hell's hottest fire,
Their gnashing, scorn, scorn of a world,
Against its votaries may be hurled,
All-maddening voices rend the air,
Weird, ghostly specters shriek despair,
Eternal battle, war declare,
All solace-founts be sealed of Time,—
Faith, Faith still spreads her wings sublime;
Supports man's feeble, tottering clay,
With visions of a brighter day,
Deep, strong within the mortal frame,
Gives solace for the world's rude shame,
The gloomy dungeon's iron bar
Lights with a heavenly, radiant star,
The scorn of foes, Satanic guile,
Dissolves in Heaven's propitious smile,
'Mid tossing waves brings peace and calm,
Anchors man's bark by isles of balm!
Amid the endless scenes of earth,

Where fond illusions teem in birth,
One incident, it stands supreme,
Proves Faith no vain, illusive dream:—
No conjured whim, born of the brain,
An ignis fatuus, meteor reign,
Dazzling, then vanishing in air,
Leaving behind no blessing rare.
A Wanderer, so style Him here,
To myriad millions precious, dear,
To Time a stranger, all unknown,
From babe to man, of sorrows grown,
From realms untraveled by the sun,
Vicarious mission came to run,
To suffer, toil, in anguish die,
That He might lift the lowly high,
Fulfil Eternal counsels wise,
With many mansions in the skies,
A church create, purged by His blood,
A spotless trophy give to God!
Mysterious Messenger of Life!
Calmer of passions, noise and strife,
By high, immortal, heavenly art,
Enlightener of the human heart,
Subduer of rebellious will,

Hard adamant made soft to feel:
Knowledge a universal book,
Omnipotence in every look!
Wisdom unbounded by a span,
Truth which the universe outran,
Dominion, Power, unchecked by bound,
In holiness, high, deep, profound,
Grace, Goodness, Majesty, unknown,
Great bleeding Lamb, from Heaven's high
    throne!
Justice eternal, without stain,
Love, Infinite, that breaks man's chain,
Speech such as mortals never spoke,
A voice at which the dead awoke!
A Presence veiled, before whose ray
The darkest night turns luminous day,—
Creation dazzled at the sight,
Astonished at the Lord of Light!
The Wonderful! great Counsellor!
The mighty God forevermore,
Great Prince of Peace, mighty Father,
The everlasting, mighty God,
Who flung creation's realms abroad!
Prophet, Revealer of all Time,

Forerunning ages grand, sublime,
His soul vast fount of quenchless fire,
To do Heaven's will, his vast desire.
He seeks the lost, the sons of shame,
The blind He cures, makes whole the lame.
The deaf restores, the palsied heals,
Heaven's sovereign will to earth reveals ;—
Works mighty miracles of power,
Sends tides of joy through Time's dark hour,
Tired, weary souls gives needed rest,
Comforts, supports, the sad, distressed,
The hardest lot gilds with joy's beam,
Heals guilt, deep woe, by love supreme.
Strange, wondrous Being !—little child
Takes to his bosom, on it smiled,
Blesses, holds up a pattern fair,
Bright key to Heaven's great glories rare,—
The mother's flowing crystal tear
More precious, prized, than rubies dear,
The incense of a grateful heart,
Treasure no Ophir's mines impart ;
Great Son Incarnate, Heaven's true love,
Sent from the worlds of Light above,
He lights the earth with love's pure fire,

Hearts that grow faint bids never tire
In the great race for virtue, good,
Glory immortal, spiritual food;—
Sustains by Love's ambrosial sense,
Of higher, sweeter recompense,—
Heaven's legacy of Love bequeathes,
Dark Time with Glory's garland wreathes;
From Time's cloud-draped, uncertain day
To God's high throne casts up highway,—
The way earth's ransomed millions tread,
Palms, crowns, Heaven's blessings on their
    head!
Blest way, where lions never roar,
Where headlong torrents never pour
Engulphing mischiefs,—opened door
To Heaven's sweet, balmy, odorous shore,—
Where thief, where bandit come not nigh;
Sorrow's dark tears forever dry,
As on the Christ is fixed each eye!
Great complex Mystery! God in man!
Mystery that solves Redemption's plan,
Begotten of the Father, born
To build on Time new purple morn,
Kingdom of darkness take away,

Succeed by love's enrapturing sway.
He comes a world to fill with peace,
From sin, from ruin give release,
Restore the ancient union broke,
Break Satan's grinding, galling yoke,
With balm all wounded spirits bind,
By Faith, Obedience, rule mankind!
Alas! for benison so grand,
See turned against Him every hand,
Dark eyes of vengeance lurid, gleam,
Hell's hostile banners flout and stream,
Volumes of wrath dart bickering flame,
Blasphemy scoffs, reviles his name;
Disowned of men, by demons dire,
Pursued by fiendish malice, ire,
Passions unloosed in reckless stride,
Assailed, He groans up Cavalry's side,
Proud scribe, revengeful Pharisee,
Delivering to the fatal tree;—
A world in arms, convulsed and torn,
He to vile martyrdom is borne,
A martyrdom of horror, shame,
Sin's monster pride to check and tame,
Heaven's amnesty to man proclaim,

Great martyrdom of torturing pain,
Opening Love's, Mercy's, endless reign,
Pardon, acceptance, through His blood,
Man reinstated with his God!
Shiloh's sweet Star, Almighty Love,
Redeemer from the realms above,
Lo! on the cross, He, groaning, dies!
Nature; deep-shuddering, shuts her eyes,
The rocks, they rend,—loud thunders roll,
Heaven's axle shakes from pole to pole,
Creation, anguished, heaves a sigh,
That her Great Lord, thus mocked, must die!
But O, what mystery!—triumph great,
In that terrific grasp of Fate!
Ere Time's foundations, massive, strong,
Angels had hymned Him in their song,
Prophets foretold, on burning lyre,
Great Muse had sung, with rapturous fire,
Traced on Heaven's scroll of living light,
Nations' Deliverer, their Delight!
Alpha, Omega, Star, bright Sun,
Whence future ages date and run!
'Twas for the joy that went before,
Faith, our Great Lord, in death, upbore,

There He the realms of Satan tore,
Gave pledge to Truth forevermore,
Broke the usurper's deadly sway,
His clanking bolts hurled far away,
Gaunt King of Terrors seized his prey ;—
Bursting the cold, the rocky tomb,
Hell, devils, Death, He smites with doom,—
With shout, up to His Father's side
Ascending, comes through empires wide,
His kingdom,—banners through the air
Waving with shout, with song and prayer!
Kingdom than earth more beauteous, dear,
Whose building brought the Pilgrims here!
Kingdom of jasper, emerald hue,
Trailing sweet twilight fringes through
Dark ages,—from whose brightening view
Flash sparkling gems each sunset, sunrise
        new,
With purple, crimson, amber bright,
Tinging dark shadows of the night,
Spreading their dusky, somber folds,
Pierced by the starry trains of worlds,—
From whose forefront flash peaks of day,
Where roseate icebergs melt away,

Where fields in bloom, all smiling lay,
All wiles, all deserts, warm with ray
From Beauty's cheek, Love's golden way,
Zoning all things with magic sway
Of bliss, of rapture's ecstacy,
While tides of deepening radiance pour,
Lighting the lands, each island shore!
Omnipotence and Faith, in One,
Light of the universe, its Sun!
His kingdom comes, in power to reign,
His, who was for Redemption slain!
By Faith in travail, He could see
Earth by His sacrifice made free,
The ponderous structures power had built,
The seas of blood in battle spilt,
The gorgeous pomps of pagan pride,
Base superstitions, far and wide,
Dark, horrid list of customs vile,
Abominations that defile,
All low, all groveling, monstrous things,
Exchanged for peace, salvation brings,
Fair Beauty, Innocence, sweet Truth,
Garlanding with perennial youth!
Great light of prophecy, sublime,

Eternity's sole gift to Time,
They who in his pure footsteps trod,
As bowed his head, found Him a God!
The slumbering dead to life awoke,
Sin's fatal cords he sundered, broke;
And while his reign but half begun
Shines like the morning's cloudless sun,
They who by Faith, make Him their all.
Through ages find their fetters fall,
Redeemer mighty, he who trod,
Great wine-press of the wrath of God,
Appeased Heaven's Justice, righteous claim,
Despising ignominies, shame,
To ope through his own blood the way
To everlasting realms of day;
Prepare white thrones, in splendor dressed,
Seats for Heaven's white-robed, sainted, bless'd!
Faith points to Him, the sacrifice,
Through whose shed blood the pathway lies,
Bows to his scepter, owns Him chief,
Through whom alone, earth finds relief
From heavy guilt, from deepest woes;
Tasting of joy whose stream e'er flows,
Drinks at the fount of quenchless Love,

Its tribes made meet for Heaven above!
That glorious Prince, Immanuel, God,
Was with the Pilgrims when they trod
The mountain wave, the lonely strand,
Thoughtful,—who for the ages planned,
Invisible, yet ever near,
To strengthen hope, allay each fear,
To prompt, direct, to guide, inspire,
Supply life's wastes with heavenly fire,
Invigorate, their wants supply,
Forsook not, 'till when called on high,
Their upward way proud to attend,
His promise keeping to the end!
His coming reign through Faith they saw,
The earth in homage to his law,
Lift its bowed head, 'mid deepening light,
Enwrapt in splendors, Heavenly bright!
Truth, long defamed, oppressed, at last
Win triumphs, conquests, unsurpassed,—
Progress, unfettered, wise, profound,
Scatter its royal blessings 'round;—
The lands in unity, in peace,
One anthem-strain without surcease,
Rolled by the nations, far and wide.

18

From valley, from each mountain side,
From lake, from river, ocean, plain,
Re-echoed back from Heaven again,
Swelling in rapturous concords clear,
That break through Time, through Heaven's
    vast sphere,
Telling that woe is ended, past,
That victory, triumph, come at last ;—
That garland virtues sweet shall flower,
Great vices crumble, lose their power,
To dismal wrongs come long surcease,
The world be warmed, with golden fleece,
New pageants deck the path of Time,
'Mid revolutions grand, sublime;
Art, Beauty, smile in freshening bloom,
New loveliness deck e'en the tomb,
Prosperities come unsurpassed,—
Heaven's blessings fall, rich, bounteous, fast !
Thanks from afar, loud, loud resound,
Earth, earth becomes all hallowed ground !
Faith, 'tis Redemption makes it grand,
Expedient, Heaven's deep counsel planned,
Vast scheme, the finite sees not through,
With heights, with depths, vast openings new,

Tracing all worlds, all tracts of Time,
With evolutions grand, sublime,
Past, Present, with the Future blends,
Time's blinding films, earth's shackles rends;
Apostasies, rebellions, feud,
Supplants by high, enduring good.
Sin's monster violences, aim,
God to dethrone, blot out his name,
High, low, the great, the small, to doom,
Give death for life, make earth a tomb.
Puts 'neath its ban, dooms with decay,
Lighting the worlds with quenchless ray
Of Life, of Glory, with a Power,
Unmeasured by Time's fleeting hour,
In an eternal splendor bright,
A day eternal with no night,
Filling all realms with deepening light!
Redemption that Heaven's silence broke,
Angel, archangel, voices spoke,
The hierarchies eldest born,
Who broke the Dragon's battering horn,
Warring in Heaven, th' accuser hurled,
From Heaven's battlements, to world
Of nether darkness, penal fire,

Who durst omnipotence aspire,
They victory's standards wave, shout, sing,
Make Heaven's vast concave echo, ring,
Hosannas pealing anthem strains,
Poured o'er all bright celestial plains,
Caught up by all the realms afar,
Where moves a planet, shines a star,—
Where systems congregate, and roll,
Earth, every land, equator, pole,
Great sea, the depths, beneath, above,
The universe in tones of Love,
Hymning the Great Creator's praise,
The mystery darting quenchless rays,
From ages, generations sealed,
In the Incarnate Son, revealed!
Redemption, that Heaven's axel turns,
A vestal fire, forever burns,
The base on which all worlds revolve,
Foundations, where all problems solve,
From primal time, to latest day,
Urging, by prodigies, its way,
By miracles, upheavals, strong,
Rolling the centuries dim, along,
With deepening power, increasing light,

Vast empires crushing in its might,
Their fragments garnering into one,
That might be born Heaven's mighty Son !
For Him all prophet symbols blaze,
The focus of their myriad rays,
In Him all epochs, cycles, meet,
The universe, in Him, complete!
Redemption, eldest of God's plans,
Though Heaven fall, whose pillar stands,
Breaking with light of endless morn,—
For which all covenants were born,
All dispensations vast and wise,
Economies that Time supplies,
Stupendous revolutions, grand,
Great bow of promise to each land,
The fiery arch, round Eden's gate,
When our first parents desolate,
For their great sin, were banished thence,
To be regained by penitence,
By Faith in One, unborn to be,
Restorer of humanity,
The nations unify and free!
Redemption, Love's vast, solar beam,
For which its banners wave and stream,

All crowns of earth, scepters, are flung,
In trophy,—while new song is sung,
Myriads on myriads, marshaled strong,
To roll its anthem-peals along,
Th' eternal archway of the skies,
Where happiness, where glory lies.
There, on a sea of glass and fire,
Where thousand thousands strike the lyre,
Heaven's seals all breaking to the last,
'Mid earthquake, voices unsurpassed,
Shall burst those wonders vast, sublime,
Before which fades recorded Time!
Wonders of Light, of Love, of Power,
At which immortal joys shall tower,
The Universe, Redemption's flower,
Sending sweet fragrance to each star,
To every world that rolls afar,
Sin's darkening shadow on God's throne,
Dissolve, in Heaven's all-blushing zone,
With dire eclipse, no more to fall,
Deliverance, triumph, starring all!

Redemption! Heaven's all-mighty, endless
    scheme,

Inlaid with Light, with Love, with Power su-
  preme,
Mightier, Oh, far! grander, more matchless,
  dear,
Than aught in human sphere,—
On that the ages poise, they grandly soar,
Great Past, faint prelude to its breaking light,—
When Paradise was lost
At Heaven's infinite cost,
It hope-lights gave Time's desolate, ravaged
  shore!
Pledged Great Redeemer, One to die,
Embraced to waft the doomed high,
That glory might succeed to endless night!
'Tis that, lo! now, wakes harps of rapturous
  praise,
Inspires with gratitude, thanksgiving, love,
While myriads, peans louder yet shall raise,
In harmony with heaven above,
Tell how the war in heaven arose,
Its tragic opening, drama close,
How Lucifer, angelic, mighty, strong,
Marshalled grim hosts, battling for ancient
  wrong,

With horrid front, in dire array,
Before the Sons of Light gave way,
Their Leader, unsurpassed, supreme,
Flashing heaven's central beam,—
Christ the Annointed, Heaven's great sun to
    rise
Within new bounds, terrestrial world,
Flash day-beams through mid-nighted, terrene
    skies,
Love, Truth all-mighty, their great banners high
    unfurled,
Bring day-springs grand, aye, sweeter, more
    sublime,
Than known in realms of Time,—
Its murky boundaries, with heavenly light im-
    pearl'd !
Redemption now, e'en now, blest voices wake,
Its mission, chains, all bonds, to sunder, break,
Onward shall speed, with giant tread shall
    steal,
Burst, burst with deepening, loudening anthem
    peal,
Grander to grow,—as violences cease,
O'erturning Sin's blasphemous, horrid reign,

'Mid deepening harmonies of love and peace,
On land, o'er heaving main,
Bringing eternal Jubilee,
Rolling vast, sparkling, swelling tide,
The Universe from side to farthest side,
Of evil long shall free !
Annihilate dark ill,
With diapasons fill,
Spreading God's light serene,
New songs of love uprising,
E'en angel ears surprising,
In origin, development, so grand,
By Goodness, Wisdom infinite, planned,
Eternity's new joy,
Heaven's hosts through ceaseless ages
    shall employ !

Redemption, 'twas for that " I Am," hath spoke,
God, His eternal silences hath broke,
His moral government by Hell assailed,
By Mercy hath prevailed,—
Law, law Divine, pure in its first estate,
Running, untarnished, all the centuries through,
Supremely Great,—th' All-Wise,

Love's final method tries;—

His justice spotless, nothing to abate,

His Holiness, vast, mighty, deepening stream,

Darting its purged, its purging beam,

He breaks His final seal, gives cov'nants new!

Lo! spring dread earthquakes, voices, thunders
　　roll,

Great waves uprise,—toss to the farthest
　　shore,

Creation trembles to the distant pole,

Heaven opes Love's starry door,—

Comes the great hour of waking bliss,

On Earth good will, an endless peace;

On sovereign Law, from out th' eternal skies,

Fall Mercy's sweet, enlustering, new-born dyes,

Hope's anxious vision thrills and warms,

No more to come doom's vengeful storms,—

Breaks Time's unstarred, oblivious night,

With Heaven's full-orbing Light,—

Great Light that radiates, illumes, to build,

In mighty tides urge on resistless way,

Till Earth with deepening splendors filled,

God's boundless empire, moral government
　　shall sway,

Effulging, brightening, roll the universe around,
With shout,—with tabor's sound,
While open ne'er to close, portals of endless
    day !
Redemption, God Himself purposed, ordained,
By prophets, patriarchs, well-taught, explained,
With lightning wheels, vast, awful, as they rise,
Flaming with thick, thick, never slumbering
    eyes,
Gigantic Error crushing as they go,
Opening for Truth, its ever-brightening path,
Supplant, annihilate all wrongs and woe,
Ending dark tyrant wrath,
Imprint God's image,—Earth shall see,
Restored,—awake new songs of Heaven-born
    power,
While destinies unroll and tower,
The Universe shall free;—

> Satan's vile hosts shall fall,
> Bondage no more enthral,
> Deliverance, mighty, come,—
> God's endless cycles sweeping,
> Unknown be tears or weeping,

Love, love resound with sweetest clarion peal,

Eternity new joys reveal,
Unending be its praise,
Myriads on myriads songs of rapture raise!
Redemption! Light and Life shall fling around,
The universe make holy, hallowed ground,
A finer radiance fall, transfiguring, sweet,
New, fairer forms shall greet,—
Great Past, with awful darkness covered o'er,
With sighs, with groans, laments, dark terrors,
    fear,
Of isolation, shame,
Of torturing martyr-flame,
Shall ne'er return,—be known, torment no
    more,
Deep-falling splendors on the crystal sea,
God's mighty hosts beatified shall be,
Himself their portion, smile, be ever near!
New, finer chords, with diapasons grand,
Shall vibrate at the touch of heavenly love,
New flowers shall blossom o'er immortal land,
New harmonies in concords move,
O'er-passed dark annals, storms, and woe,
With rapture every heart shall glow,
The ransomed all around new scenes shall see

New powers awake, within their bosoms free,
Far-reaching, fetterless, to scan
Th' Eternal Wisdom's crowning plan,
Disasters, sorrows, all unknown,
In blaze of Heaven's throne!
Redemption crowned, shall pour a ceaseless
    light,
Open in vistas of unending joy,
Undimmed, its destinies to wax, grow bright,
The Universe its countless myriads shall em-
    ploy,
With dateless period, on its tide shall go,
No limit, boundaries know,
With mission to renew, apostacies destroy!
At its grand triumph opening realms of Love,
The great intelligencies high, above,
In choral symphonies shall pour new song,
Rolling in diapasons thunderous strong,
Till loud re-echoed thro' the heavenly spheres,
Its melody caught up, returned from far,
Gone by these dim, these anxious, mortal
    years,—
Be heard by every star,
The New Jerusalem come down,

Blazing in gems, in rubies, sapphires bright,
Fling lusters, fadeless, on Time's passing night,
Wear an eternal crown!
  Glad, joyous in that day,
  They who now toil and pray,
  Their pleasure be supreme,
  Christ, Christ a God, confessing,
  Earth's needy poor e'er blessing,
Great magnates, grandees, they their Lord shall
  see,—
  'Mid Heaven's air, in Liberty,
  While louder still shall roll
Redemption's song, with golden chain bind
  every soul!

'Tis that makes Faith so precious, grand,
Redemption its receiving hand;—
Faith, 'tis its mighty horoscope,
Used oft by Love, fond Patience, Hope,
Sweeping th' eternal, sun-lit sky,
It brings redemption's glories nigh,
Assimilates, yields heavenly food,
Incorporates immortal good,
Life, strength imparts, creates anew,

Opes endless vistas on man's view,
Unseals the fount of heavenly light,
Gives inspiration, joy, delight,
Eases life's burdens, toils, its care,
By solace-sweets, Heaven's manna rare,
Points to beatitudes, that lie
In fields of splendor 'yond the sky,
Where, while eternal ages roll,
Ecstatic bliss shall crown the soul!
Faith, civilization, gives true life,
Plucks from foul errors wasting strife,
Antagonisms that endless wage,
Fierce battles in adulterous age.
On adamantine basis pure,
The race it plants, makes firm, secure,
Links in th' Eternal council, plan,
Where Truth and Justice lead the van,
To conflicts that shall wake mankind,
All spiritual shackles to unbind!
Faith sends, resistless, through the world,
Life-tides of power, builds one vast fold,
Where man adorned, can glorious rise,
Sweet charm, to keen archangel eyes,
Quaffing fair sweets of Heaven-born life,

Conqueror of Rage, Earth's endless strife,
It spreads white wing, dove-like it broods
O'er devastations, darkening floods,
O'er wrath, o'er ruins, fearful woes,
Sweet, flooding radiance, Glory throws,
Born 'mid the heavenly heights above,
Of God's eternal, sovereign love,
Fed, nourished, on blest food divine,
In vigor, strength, ordained to shine,
It disentangles, rends away,
Whate'er usurps unrighteous sway,
Clips foul ambition's venturous wings,
'Mid noisome pools opes crystal springs,
All mists, deep darkness, drives apace,
With heaven-born prizes crowns the race:—
Society gives bulk, gives mould,
Turns all its fruitage into gold,
Purges of feculences foul,
Of follies, atheistic scowl,
Of rancorous hate, of rampant wrong,
Inspires with joy's new-waking song,
Truth, Right, the Good, making supreme,
As earth lights with its central beam!
Lo! Faith, 'tis lode-star, guide to Time,

Its deeds unparalleled, sublime,
It cancels doubt, flashes a ray
That sins, miasma, drives away;
The darkness, gloom, that chill our sight,
Dissolve in its immortal light;
With new, creative vigor, strong,
It undermines each hoary wrong;
Makes thorn that pricked earth's wounded
    side
Bloom a sweet lily, in its pride;
Each agony of grief, despair,
It solaces with trusting prayer;
Th' enfeebled will of fallen man,
Darkened, hemmed in with narrowing span,
Devoid of good, sovereign its ills,
Renewed, with joy, with rapture thrills;
Deep to the center of each heart,
Guilt, anguish, sorrow, cease their smart,
Oblivion's streams, o'er vices roll,
While Heaven within fills all the soul!
Would you a power supremely great,
To build the social, civil state,
Give immobility and death
A living force, a vital breath,

20

From decadence, dumbness, restore,
The fading earth to fade no more,
Stir the vast stagnant pool of things,
With silver currents, crystal springs,—
Hide from the riven, bondaged earth,
Great curse of barrenness and dearth,
Cause the vast globe to fill with Life,
No more appear inglorious strife,
Blessings descend rich, bounteous, rare,
An odorous sweet pervade the air,
Each power, each agent, give control
To guard each right, maintain the whole,—
Where, where in all the earth abroad
Can that be found save Faith in God?
Of high, celestial, glorious birth,
Faith, Faith alone, has priceless worth,—
It gives new charms to lusters bright,
The earthly clothes in Heavenly light,
Transcendent intercourse restores,
Beatitudes through opened doors
Unveils, on sea of burning glass,
Pomps, pageantries, that endless pass,
In that unfading world of power,
Where man God's king, high-priest, shall tower!

Let civilizations root on high,
No longer be pollution's sty,
Where poisonous vapors upward rise,
Wafting to Heaven earth's groans and sighs;
Dread Aceldama, tears and blood,
Poured centuries long in deepening flood;
Man, grateful man, the soil shall till,
Obedient to his Maker's will;
True art, true industries inspire,
Earth warm with new, heroic fire;
Commerce shall spread her snow-white wing,
From farthest lands sweet spices bring,
Great Christian handmaid, virtuous, rare,
No wasting scourge to nations bear,—
The State shall feel no earthward shock,
Stand firm on massive crystal rock;
In georgeous majesty arrayed,
Fling far and wide protective shade,—
Power burn with vengeance 'gainst all wrong,
Protect the weak, uphold the strong;
Through government, through righteous law,
Man, new-born strength, fresh vigor draw.
Faith at its touch, e'en floating straw
Sparkles a diamond without flaw!

The dust beneath, a shining gem,
The patriots crest, a diadem !
Let Faith on Heaven clasp firm its hold,
A Midas-wand, turns all to gold;
The things that now in lowness lie,
Shall brighten with immortal dye,
In brightening hues of beauty beam,
Flash, send afar, a radiant gleam,
Of deepening light, brighter to grow,
Till splendor flood the worlds below,
Effulgence deepening, without end,
Above, beneath, around, extend,
All masks shall fall from off all eyes,
Hypocrasies, pretensions, lies,
A kingdom glorious then shall rise,
Hated by fools, loved by the wise,
Baseness and crime be overthrown,
Truth sit supreme upon her throne.
From North, from South, from East, from West,
Shall peal new harmonies of rest,
The pure in heart alone, shall reign,
Of Fate nor Providence complain.
One choral song of life shall roll,
Be heard from centre to each pole,

All jarring discords, rending Time,
Be lost in melodies sublime;
Great brotherhood of man appear,
Sweet Sabbath peace encrown the sphere!
Eternal Faith in league with Right,
The foes of truth shall put to flight;
Proud champion, shall e'er prevail,
Omnipotent, can never fail!
The solace, refuge of each hour,
Life's guardian Genius, conquering Power,
E'en when its journey first begun,
It shines a bright, celestial Sun.
In youth, behold! it wakes desire,
Kindles each bosom with its fire,—
When dire despondencies o'ercloud,
When Circean charms of pleasure shroud,
When misty veil of darkening air
Forbodes deep misery, pain, despair
Of human joy,—its cup o'erset
Of expectations unforgot,
Purging the vision in its light,
Dissolve the darkening glooms of night;—
It whispers, clouds shall pass away,
Dawn soon the wished-for, happy day,

Solace to pain shall quick succeed,
The hearts that now in anguish bleed
Shall fill with peace, the curtain rise,
Sweet, golden sunshine cheer all eyes!
Thus Faith, with gladness gilds its reign,
Round tearful hearts weaves golden chain,
Scatters each tribulation, woe,—
As days glide on, the seasons go,
Through its transforming, magic power,
Each steals a triumph on the hour!

Far down the steep of wreathless Time,
The bard who feels a heat sublime,
Whose numbers yet shall grandly roll,
And waft his name to either pole,
Whose searching harmonies shall thrill,
With rapture, mightiest spirits fill!
Obscurities, deep shadows fall,
His unknown energies in thrall,
Fearing to make Æonian flight,
And break the dungeon of his night.
Lo! Faith flashes a heavenly beam,
He wakes 'mid life's embosomed dream,
A new-born energy inspires;

Kindles his being's inmost fires,
He strikes the harp, the numbers steal;
Stamp his fair brow with deathless seal,
By faith he climbs the mount of fame,
Wins glory, an immortal name!

Nor less through life's descending scale,
Where want, where labors rude prevail;—
'Tis Faith 'mid gloom's desponding night,
Unwraps sweet visions, heavenly bright;
Hard, humble toil, plodding apace,
Allures by fortune's brighter race,
Sweetens the present with the joy
That nobler tasks shall soon employ;
The wearied father sees his son
Advanced in honor's path to run,
Plucking grand laurels, wreathe his brow,
Blesses his stars, pays Heaven his vow.
The care-worn mother sees her child,
Who pained her heart by darings wild,
A pillar grown, to tottering age,
Her fears, her sorrows, all assuage;
The happy pair, 'mid sunbeams bright,
Descend life's vale, nor fear death's night,

Assured that sorrow points the way
Through bright'ning beams to endless day!

Lo! on this isthmus dark, of Time,
Where throng, sad mem'ries, woe, and crime,
See Hymen's star go out in night,
Sweet, fond affection wither, blight,
Death pluck life's branches, budding, fair,
No heart from sorrow, anguish, spare;
See love, true friendship, dim, grow dark,
Frail innocence, calumny's mark;
See rapturing thoughts of early bliss
Wreck in the shade of loneliness,—
Lover and loved sped swift away,
Life one dark, dismal, cloudy day;—
The beauteous bride one hour, life's sun,
The next, her mortal journey run,
Earth's fairest prize, a meteor flown,
Connubial happiness unknown;
Forced, sad, reluctant, soon to part,
See her fond mate, a broken heart,
In solitude walk, muse, alone,
Sigh with a tear, and heave a groan!
His country calls,—he takes the sword,

Moistens the urn, for one adored,
On glittering steed, in prancing mein,
He fearless rides, till foe is seen;—
Foremost grand champion on the field,
He falls, his country's triumph sealed,—
No hand to smoothe the aching brow,
Or soothe life's ebbing current's flow,
To pile rude stone, sweet dirges pour,
The agonies of nature o'er!
None, none, through friendship, to draw near,
No voice to speak his memory dear,
Tell the proud tale to fellow-man,
Here hero sleeps who led the van,
Where courage, valor, led the way
To freedom, Glory's brightest day!
But winds and waves shall requiems roll,
Fame speak his deeds to either pole,
Earth cannot lose a hero-soul!
Beyond Time's blight, its battle-storm,
Renewed shall be the lover's form,
Two blended hearts by love made one,
A high immortal race shall run;—
And while proud ages drop their tear
Around the conquering hero's bier,

21

And weep for him, for her so dear,
Faith, Faith, shall its proud scepter wave,
And tell of life beyond the grave !
Thus, through the varying walks of life,
Faith drops her smiles, with blessings rife,—
Comes in the hour of pain, despair,
Soothes human sorrows, woe and care.
When darkness sullens into gloom,
When trials throng with threat'ning doom,
When dire misfortunes rob of joy,
When Heaven-lit Hope mingles alloy,
And picturing scenes of fancied bliss
Blight, life but one vast weariness,
When mightiest passions strive and rage,
And Doubt and Fear dread conflicts wage,
When pride, ambition, rampant, strong,
Impel to paths of vice and wrong,
Error flinging deceptive light,
To plunge in ruin's blackening night,
Back from the vortex, Faith can hold,
Gather within Truth's starry fold,
To all give light, composure, peace,
Make Eden-bright life's wilderness !
Let desolation stalk the plain,

Nature to chaos turn again,
Let maddening wheels of chariots fly,
War, lurid, paint the midnight sky,
Let Pestilence, stark Famine dire,
Bid nations, in their march, expire,
The only sovereign, safeguard, law,
Death, its eternal swinging maw,
Sackcloth with darkness deepen night,
E'en then shall break returning light!
Faith, undismayed, then tells vile man
The riven globe shall smile again,
On barren heath, on lonely plain,
Where terror, want and ruin reign,
'Mid desert wastes, vast mountains high,
Summits that prop the vaulted sky,
'Mid leafless vales, forests dark gloomed,
Where savage nations lie entomb'd,
There rose shall bud, sweet lily smile,
Nature yet charm with many a wile,
Man's wandering footsteps oft beguile.
The bee's sweet hum, the swallow's trill,
With rapturing music woodland fill,
Each flowery haunt, each sylvan dell,
With love's returning accents swell,

Sweet forms of Life all beauteous, fair,
Warble Elysian concords there!
Cities shall rise, towns, hamlets spread,
'Neath proud Advancement's giant tread,
Knowledge, new civil arts, extend,
Wealth, Science, Laws, new grandeur lend,
Taste, grand munificence, combine,
Barbarian rudeness check, refine,
Enluster, polish, deck, adorn,
The promised age of gold be born!
Light break on every waiting land,
In deepening splendors, glories grand,
Creation through her utmost bound,
Rejuvenesce, with rapture sound,
Truth, Freedom, Justice, laurels wear,
Man triumph 'neath Heaven's guardian care!
Say, Faith, eternal, grand, sublime,
Daughter of Heaven, thou child of Time,
Amid bright prophesies so fair,
Earth yet to bloom with glories rare,—
Say, these the only tidings dear,
Thou bring'st to man's expectant ear?
Given to light Time's narrow span,
To vindicate God's ways to man,

To soothe, console, sustain, make strong,
To bear these terrene ills and wrong;
Say, is thy blissful mission done,
E'er breaks Heaven's high, eternal sun?
Can there be found of soul so drear,
Who think fond beings end is here,
Living on folly, pleasure's sound,
In sensual vices plunged and drowned,
Who 'mid creation's wondrous play,
Esteem fond man, child of day!
Avaunt! base sceptics! thoughtless few,
False, false, your lifeless, soulless view,
To think this world, nature sublime,
These pomps, grand pageants, tricks of Time!
These myriad forms of life, so fair,
Mere accidents, devoid of care;
These sparkling worlds, that round us roll,
No guardian, no final goal,
Careering blind through empty space,
Aimless, uncaused, their dazzling race;—
This Order, Harmony, supreme,
Unvisited by Reason's beam;
Earth, Time, but bubble, empty dream,
All things afloat, their current, stream,

Unknown,—but flash,—a meteor gleam,
Phantasmagoria, soon to fall,
O'erpower, whelm, crush and ruin all!
Man, but an embryo spark of fire,
A lighted taper, soon t' expire,
Th' immortal spirit, heavenly bright,
But phantom breath, to sink in night,
Like beast to perish, feel decay,
From consciousness, be torn away,—
No Destiny, no Race to run,
Beyond Time's clouded, setting sun,
In heavenlier lands, worlds high, unknown,
To live, while God maintains his throne!
Then why at flitting shadows start,
Ye blind, of proud, deceptive heart;—
Why, when God's judgments, march severe,
Yield ye, like ghosts, to paleness, fear;—
Why when the vivid lightnings play,
Frighten and scare, toss with dismay,
When fearful earthquakes spring the ground,
Heave mountain fastnesses around,
When dire tornadoes sweep through air,
Why offer forced, reluctant prayer;
Why mock, then bow the quivering knee,

Plead Heaven from peril's doom to free?
False, fugitive, your shaken boast,
'Mid sharp disasters, strangely tossed,
Base, cowardly fools! quivering, aghast,
When giant danger marches past,
There is no Atheism then,
Base infidels, believing men!
Were there no future prospects grand,
Darkness, deep night, would shroud each land;
Were man but being of a day,
Tasting vain joys to pass away,
Feeling this pulse-tide of a world
Quicken, then dashed, to ruin hurled,
Life's mutual hopes abundant share,
Then blight, vanish 'mid empty air
His aspirations, glowing thought,
Hemmed in by unstarred, earthly lot,
No opening paths for him to soar,
Plume fancy's pinions evermore;
Give to imagination's powers
To revel 'mid Elysian bowers,
'Mid scenes of light, in rapture feel,
Eternal sunshine round him steal,
The earthly tasks, labors, laid down,

For Heaven's bright, starry, dazzling crown !
Then curse the hour that gave him birth,
Time false, fantastic mummery, mirth,
Delusion, sham, a groveling show,
Senses bewildering overflow,
The lovely flowers of Life that bloom,
All emptiness, a waste perfume,
Nature, her lusters, pageants, sweet,
False, false her voices, echoes, fleet,—
Then bid her pulse quick cease to beat,
Take back this momentary heat,
This quenchless ardor, quenchless flame
Of mocking life, mistaken name !
Amid a wilderness of woes,
Give chance-created forms repose,
Friends cease to mourn, to sorrow, weep ;
If death be an eternal sleep,
The sepulcher man's final goal,
O'er which oblivion's waters roll !
Not thus they taught, great Pilgrim sires ;
Man burns with Heaven's immortal fires,
With its pure radiance, kindles bright,
For endless scenes of joy, delight ;
No momentary being planned,

His powers august, amazing, grand,
A miracle of wondrous skill,
Of conscience, Reason, Freedom, will,
To walk high paths, lift peerless eye,
Scan splendors bright beyond the sky,
In blissful hope, that one day there
He Glory's diadem crown shall wear !
And yet at death, who would not start,—
Man feels of sundering ties the smart,
When nature's tender cords are riven,
The soul, by pain, to frenzy driven,
When earthly light 'mid anguish fades,
And round are spread death's dismal shades,
O then, to bid final adieu,
Mysterious paths, unknown, pursue,
No friend, no kindred soul to cheer,
Light up the mortal passage drear,
Untended, helpless, faint, alone,
Compelled to leap for worlds unknown,—
Who would not shiver on the brink,
Feel all his mortal courage sink !
Lo ! then a voice breaks loud and clear,
A voice from Heaven's eternal sphere,
Sweet, as blest sounds from spicy fields,

That mortal terrors, anguish, heals;—
Faith lights the shadowy, starless gloom,
Bursts marble, adamantine tomb,
Points to the realms of living Light,
Immortal worlds, celestial, bright;
From these dark scenes of death, despair,
Flings wide the gates to Glory there!
There, where eternal splendors roll,
Where rapture's fire warms every soul,
Where seraph tongues their notes employ
To kindle love's perennial joy,
Bids each winged spirit, fearless, turn,
Triumphant, death's dark horrors spurn,
Gaze on sweet mansions in the skies,
Heaven's blissful immortalities;
High, everlasting, blest abode,
The Saints' sweet home, palace of God!
Though in the dust the body lie,
The soul shall walk that palace high,
Encrowned a king, in royal state,
Outshining earthly conquerors great;
Enfranchised, soar, in grandeurs rise,
Bask in the light that never dies;
The race of Time, feebly begun,

There in immortal vigor run!
And when this vast, decaying frame,
With torch funereal lights to flame,
When fires of ether bright shall glow,
And madness seize on all below,
When stars shall rush amid the sky,
And spheres from traveled orbits fly,
Yon pensile orb, so glorious bright,
The sun go out in endless night,
And crack of doom, with horror vast,
Ruin's sharp plough-share drives at last,—
Amid the crash of falling worlds,
O'er rising dead, Faith's scroll unfurls!
Then, then proud man on wings sublime
She lifts, to tower o'er Nature, Time,
Trace to the source of Light, his way,
His final goal, eternal day!
The earthly, mortal changes done,
The race of Time completed, run,
'Tis her's the spirit to prepare,
Raise to immortal converse there;—
There lift the dimning curtain, veil,
Where darkness, night, no more assail,
Point the sweet landscapes, in the skies,

Of balmy splendor, purple dyes,
Enchantment to superior eyes,—
Regions where Glory's beams surprise,
Land that in endless verdure lies,
Where everlasting summits rise,
Roseate in grandeur, flaming bright,
Joy to cherubic-angel sight;
Far-sweeping vistas, opening grand,
Blazing in gems, with rainbow spanned,
Of sweet, ethereal, deep'ning glow;
Sweet land, where crystal waters flow,
Where pleasures, change, nor dimness know;
The home, the fount of Being, where
Beauty unveils all graces rare,
Where anthem-peals of love loud roll,
And Heaven's fruition crowns the soul!

O, wondrous Faith! without thy aid
Mankind of shadows were afraid;
Firm on no base of sheltering rock,
Fancy would sport, and endless mock;
Rude, conjuring forms of terror dire,
Extinguish Hope's celestial fire,
Man's half-enlightened, trembling form,

Rude prey to error's blackening storm !
Say, without Faith, its quickening power,
What were proud man, but for an hour
A shadow, vapor, born to die,
A whisper, groan, an ending sigh !
Let him but touch Faith's magic wand,
Lo ! deathless energies expand,
On Glory's mount he takes his stand,
Hears harmonies, infinite, sweep,
Wakes from his fitful, mortal sleep,
The spark that lights his being here,
Undimm'd, to burn through endless year !
O, Muse, diversified thy strain,
Yet let not critic dare complain.
What theme so just, so congruous, fair,
Great Pilgrim honors to declare?
Not Eneas, seeking Latium's coast,
Driven by gales, by sea-storms tossed,
Founding an iron empire, grand,
The wonder, conqueror of each land,
Absorbing dynasties, with power
O'er prostrate realms to rise and tower,
Crush the vast world, by Fate's dread doom,
Imperial, martial, pagan Rome !

Assyrian, Persian, elder born,
Empires that flourished near Time's morn ;—
Not of Achilles' dreadful wrath,
That paints the Grecian hero path,
Do I now sing,—a later day,
The shadows, glooms, dissolved away,—
Mightier than eldest, primal Time,
Grander in deeds, waxing sublime,
Pouring sweet splendors o'er a world,
'Neath Freedom's starry flag unfurled ;
Great Pilgrim heroes unsurpassed,
No rivaling peers through all the Past !
Great age of Faith by them begun,
Sublimer grows each setting sun,
Disjointed fragments, systems wild,
Parts that in true proportions smiled,
Of symmetries, of grandeurs shorn,
With elements of life re-born,
Now unify, affiliate, blend,
To higher gravitations tend.
Faith solves the riddle of the world,
Chaos turns order, systems whirled
With aimless speed through empty air,
Feel Heaven's high hand, its guardian care,

Bright dazzling orbs that round us roll,
But parts of one stupendous whole;
Whose paths are traced, fixed, fixed their goal,
Their order, harmony, supreme,
Lit by Heaven's radiant, quenchless beam,—
These myriad elements combined,
All governed by th' Eternal Mind;
The atoms in their ceaseless turn,
The mystic lights that round us burn,
The seasons grand, their golden hours,
Sweet sunshine, the refreshing showers,
Nature, with all her radiant host, .
The springing bud, autumnal frost,
Earth's mighty forces, sky and air,
In one divine protection share!
Guarding alike the moral world,
When empires rise, to ruin hurled,
When dynasties, when kingdoms break,
And civil earthquakes nations shake,
When darkness, treachery, guilt and crime
With revolutions startle Time,
Summoning proud man to deeds sublime,
Oppressed, long struggling to be free,
He holds thy gates, Thermopylæ!

Earth one vast mount of sacrifice,
Faith, pointing heroes to the skies,
Telling fond man Heaven hears his cries,
That cause of Justice never dies,
Whether, with armor girded on,
He stands the shock at Marathon,
At Salamis, on classic wave,
Or 'neath Rome's eagles waxes brave,
Maintains the centuries' long, long fight,
For Freedom, man's God-given birthright,—
Or, struggling still, for conquests grand,
On modern ground he takes his stand,
Rivals the Roman, Spartan band,
At Culloden, on Bunker's height,
In Glory's splendor flaming, bright,—
All battle-fields grow holy ground
Where man hath fetters, chains, unbound,
Through centuries,—Time's deepening stream,
Lit by Heaven's piercing, purging beam,
Bursting his thraldom, high to rise,
Claim nobler birthright in the skies!
An age of Faith, lo! Time, transforms!
The mountain summits, hung with storms,
The misty vales, with night o'ercast,

Glow in new splendors, unsurpassed ;—
A radiance falls from out the sky,
Purer than earth-born beams supply,
Tracing new beauties in each line,
Making pale forms divinely shine.
'Neath holier light, with quickened tread,
Progress, Advancement, lift their head;
Effulgence breaks on every shore,
Light beams intense, creation o'er;
New, wondrous arts unlock their store.
Rare mines, sweet gems of golden ore;
New spiritual forces vast, refined,
Stir, build, advance, exalt mankind,
Open vast fields of reason, thought,
Of boundless mental wealth unwrought,
That summon man's immortal zeal,
Creative powers to carve, unseal,
New destinies of Light and Love,
In harmony with Heaven above!
New honors bud, comes virtuous fame,
Lights, lights the world, Redemption's flame !
All things o'erarch with scenes more bright,
Find welcome, give man new delight;
New orbs mysterious break afar,
24

Unveil bright spheres, with dazzling star,
Heaven's zodiac, with Light transforms,
From thrones of day, smile heavenly forms;
Nature, creation, earth and Time,
Clothe in magnificence sublime;
An august presence awes the world,
Thrones, scepters, kingdoms, tyrants, hurled
As lightnings flash from upper sky,
Thus quick they fall, in ruins lie.
Reason, bright Truth, conquering stern Might,
Dawns Time's great age of Justice, Right,
Eternal principles command,
Strike deepening root in every land,—
Marshalls earth's mighty hero band,
A mightier host than ever trod
Time's giddy stage, the host of God,
Grappling with error that hath bound
The soaring spirit to the ground,
Imbruted energies of fire,
Quenched man's immortal, proud desire,
Palled his keen vision, piercing, bright,
In sackcloth, gloom, appalling night,
Made intellect, Heaven's purest breath,
Dull with the clogging damps of death;

Dissolving temples God hath built,
His glorious shrines, by damning guilt!
Lo! 'long the lands deep watchword rolls,
It rouses heaven-born, hero-souls;
Legions innumerable arise,
March, countermarch, th' arch fiend surprise;
They who for Truth, true Glory, dare,
Bright burnished weapons lo! they wear,—
Fast gathering 'long the hills of Time,
For conquests, victories, grand, sublime,
In squadrons bright, they rapid move,
Stirred by the trumpet tones of Love,—
Foul prejudices flung away,
They hail Perfection's rapturous day,
No feuds dark bickering for the fray,
Filled now with hope, now with dismay,
With vain maneuverings selfish play;—
Deep love of God, love, love for man,
Leads on the thickening, serried van;
While adverse hosts, with leering eye,
The bright'ning ranks, trembling espy,
Lo! see the columns, soon to close,
On Armageddon's field of woes,
Great field of prophecy, of fate,

Where combatants, with hope elate,
Shall strive for virtue, strive for wrong,
Puissant, stand in conflict long,
Earth's final battle fought for fame,
For Glory's prize, or endless shame!
When Heaven's loud trump shall shake the
    the sky,
The thickening banners lifted high,
Truth's starry folds o'er all shall lie,
As Faith's bright shield is passing by,
With nerveless grasp, deep groan, and sigh,
Truth's beaten foes in rout shall fly,
Great conflict end, and error die;
God's purpose from eternity,
To star Time's course with victory,
When the last conflict shall be won,
E'er nature pass, or sets her sun!
The stormiest winds that battle blow,
Rush, thwart all hemispheres and go
Laying dynasties, kingdoms, low,
All continents, all isles, that lie
In ruins black, as they go by,
Be calmed, serene, all pure the air,
Time's final sunset, glorious, fair!

Man, man shall bow the humble knee,
Confess 'twas God who makes him free;
He, soon to rise, and upward soar,
Love, mercy, endless, praise, adore;
On Heaven's sweet, balmy, perfumed shore
The struggle here by Faith begun
End, when bright Glory's mount is won!
Such the great conflict of the earth,
From Nature's fair, immortal birth,
Mankind in bondage from the Fall,
Faith conquers, triumphs over all,—
Brings back the golden age of Time,
Crowns earth with blessings grand, sublime,
Renews, transforms, points the bright way
To heavenly glories, endless day!

Then let the world to Faith bow down,
Put on its radiant, star-bright crown,
Walk the bright, star-lit, heavenly road
That leads to happiness and God!
Wild torrents roll, fierce winds still blow,
Dire earthquakes shake these realms below,
Foul, wide-mouthed Vengeance walks abroad,
Dark, hellish hate would unthrone God,

Envy still lingers in man's breast,
Rude passion's fire disturbs his rest;
But while the blazing thunders roll,
And Nature trembles to her pole,
While fierce tornadoes blast and sweep,
The nations sigh, o'er ruins weep,
Earth's gravitation's downward force,
'Tis Faith arrests, gives upward course!

Not Newton, with his star-smit soul,
Darting through space, where planets roll,
From fallen apple, as it lie,
Impelled to seek the mystic tie
That binds the universe around,
In order, harmonies profound,
Made such discovery of Heaven's law,
With kindred magnet-power to draw
To one grand center, give control,
Of parts in one united whole,
Till at the cross he bowed his heart,
There felt Faith's pulse-tides quick'ning start!
Faith, 'tis philosophy in love,
Distills with life from Heaven above,
It brings all wounded bosoms rest,

Relief from pain, when sore distressed;
Forever on Heaven's strength relies,
In needy hour all good supplies;
When day-dreams, apathy, beguile,
It prompts, rebukes, with Sovereign smile;
Truth's lamp it causes bright to shine,
Ray with effulgence sweet, divine;
Lures by vast motives, visions rare,
Girds mightiest souls, to do, and dare;
Genius it fires with holiest aim,
Fills Nature's temple with a flame
Of sacred incense, e'er to rise;
The humble heart, God's sacrifice,
The contrite soul, submissive will,
Deigns with the richest gifts to fill,
Blesses the lowly, cheers the meek,
The stammering tongue it helps to speak,
Sees, dim-reflected in each star,
A brighter glory, beaming far;
All things grow hallowed in its light,
Transform, and glow in radiance bright,
Beauties immortal, in its eye,
It hails Time's omens, as they fly;
Each mellowing tint, of magic dye,

Proclaims Christ's march to victory ;
When hastened by its power sublime,
Triumph shall gild the goal of Time !
With optics science never knew,
It scans God's works, His mercies through ;
Beyond these wasting, crumbling spheres,
The roll of centuries, gliding years,
The universe sees spiral turn,
To where God's mighty altars burn ;—
The mighty void, tempestuous deep,
Bridges where trailing comets sweep,
Where starry isles, vast systems break,
Where suns eclipse in ruin's wake,
Where blustering chaos pours fierce tide
Of devastation, dark and wide,
Where ghostly forms in terror speak,
And weird, grim specters, horrid shriek,
Where grizzly fiends, with daring breath,
Mock at the drifting piles of death,
Nature, tenantless, through her sphere,
A riven tomb, void sepulcher,
Across th' oblivious, darkening flood
Of groans and sighs, Time's sea of blood,
Beyond the sunless, starless sky,

To where bright lands immortal lie,
Points to the sapphire, pearl on high,
Terrace on terrace, beauteous, grand,
In Glory's brightest sunbeams spanned !
There, as it waves its wand, is seen,
Vast realms in high celestial sheen,
A city's glistening towers and spires,
Vast temple, with its altar-fires,
Huge battlements, in Glory bright,
Pinnacles flashing heavenly light,
Palaces, mansions, royal, fair,
Pillars, vast columns, domes, mid air
Of ceaseless light, effulgence, where
With frontal gems all beauties blend
In deepening splendor without end !
Sweet paradise ! the home of God,
The saints' perpetual, blest abode,
Where pain, death, sorrow, none e'er know,
Where life's pure crystal waters flow,
Bliss, rapture, joy, unstained by woe,
Knowledge, wisdom, endless to grow,
Realms stainless, pure as driven snow !
For that proud Faith, the Pilgrims came,
They light the ages with its flame,

25

Scorning all yokes, fetters that bind
Th' immortal, quickening, soaring mind,
Heaven's reflex image, purged and free,
They triumph everlastingly!

The Pilgrim Fathers are not dead,
They move in Phalanx overhead;
Loosed from these narrow bounds of Time,
New conquests wait their steps sublime;
Their armor bright they lay not down,
Wearing immortal conqueror's crown;
Great work of heroes just begun,
As breaks Heaven's bright unclouded sun!
Fancy still sees them 'neath Heaven's care,
In mighty conflicts grandly dare,—
With waving plumes in robes of light,
The Heavenly powers supreme delight!
Their charneled dust at Plymouth cold,
Their ransomed spirits mighty, bold,
'Mid heavenly strains of thunder rolled,
They brave new deeps as erst of old,
Dare deeds of virtue, Glory, Fame,
At which Time's annals blush for shame,—
On tranquil seas of crystal Light,

Eternal battles wage for Right,
For Truth, for Justice, Mercy, Love,
For them still sacrifice and strive;
New hemispheres by Faith and prayer,
Grand offerings to their Maker bear;
Foremost of all the heavenly race,
They move like lightnings through all space,
In the eternal counsels, plan,
Fulfill their mission Time began;
Crowned with the smiles of angels, God,
They tread the paths the mightiest trod,
See the last saddening glooms of night,
Blush 'mid Heaven's cloudless morning bright;
Companion of the sons of Light,
They walk high Glory's palmy way,
And triumph 'mid eternal day!

When sitting pensive, nature still,
There comes a power of loftier will,
Serener shines some radiant star,
From depths of ether dim, afar,
We feel that eyes are watching round,
With high solicitudes, profound,
Watching each movement of the mind,

Luring to labors for mankind;
We feel their presence as though near,
Though shrined in Heaven's eternal sphere!
O, from them let all patterns draw
Of Virtue, Order, Union, Law,
Seek Glory's paths, by Faith, to tread,
That we with them, th' illustrious dead,
Nature o'erpast, may upward rise,
Share the same blest eternities,
Bask in the smiles, the Love of God,
Purchased, redeemed by Christ's dear blood!

Two hundred fifty years are o'er
Since their frail bark on Plymouth's shore
Discharged the precious freight it bore,
Task theirs to hero souls assigned,
Lo! countless blessings greet mankind,—
Fetters of ages fast unbind,
Eternal garlands are entwined!
The Muse unwilling to retire,
Kindling with an unceasing fire,
Her task is done: may some grand lyre,
Centuries ahead, renew the song,
All musical, harmonious, strong,

The Pilgrim praises still prolong;
While Time shall beat its ceaseless tread,
Immortalize the glorious dead!
Immortal champions of the race,
Their glorious deeds shall ne'er efface;
Their names in living radiance bright;
E'ermore shall glow 'mid deepening light!
They strike new chords, a world they cheer;
They build, renew, transform Time's sphere;
Life's dull routine traveled from old,
Through them flashes imperial gold,—
Its usage, customs, groveling, vile,
Wear dignities beneath their smile;
With new-born power, intense, sublime,
They crown these blasted realms of Time;
To fearful night bring glorious day,
By wisdom, virtue, knowledge sway!

Niagara, awful in its roar,
Dread thundering torrent e'er shall pour,
Great Monarch! in its headlong plunge,
Laugh at the tyrant's weak revenge;
Enwreathed in mist shall sparkle gem,
Enthroned, wear nature's diadem,

Arch with its bow divinely fair,
Beauty and Power ! hold empire there!
Onward majestic e'er to stride,
Its waters swell great ocean's tide,
Shall heave and crest in every sea,
Roll on great anthem of the Free !
Great king of Day, the sun shall shine,
Flame with magnificence divine,—
Dissolve the ebon realms of night,
With beauteous, warm, creative Light;
Creation charm with unspent power,
Illume and bless Time's latest hour;
Nor till earth's gravitations die,
Ruling all worlds where'er they fly,
Shall Pilgrims mightiest of mankind,
Fail worthiest praises due to find !

They come, they come, that hero train,
O'er heaving surge, o'er bounding main,
Man's inborn rights to conquer, gain,
            Opening pearl gates of day!
They come at Duty's mighty call,
Nations asleep in endless thrall,
Through their great work their fetters fall,
            They consecrate Time's way!

Their's mightiest conquest 'neath the sun,
In Duty's path by man e'er run,
Sublime shall end as it begun,
   Great halocaust to fame,—
From Time's uplifted veil, go view
Great hero-trains, pass swiftly through,
They who to Duty faithful, true,
   Star with eternal name!

Go ask the mightiest chiefs of time,
Who trod the paths the centuries chime,
Who sleep in Glory's shroud sublime,
   To tell earth's grandest deed,—
They who at Duty's voice awoke,
For man, his chains, his bondage broke,
Who Truth's immortal accents spoke,
   And mighty nations freed!

Fierce, dreadful storms around them hung,
Their exile from oppression wrung,
Their path of trial, dark, unsung,
   Faith nerved with hero pride,—
The hurricane poured fierce its blast,
Darkness, thick gloom, deep, overcast,

Great deeds, and true, live unsurpassed,
  Build earth's great empire wide!
In Duty's light they onward hie,
Their perils, tribulations, die,
At length, beneath the Western sky,
  They bow supreme to God;—
The forests with their joys awake,
Their accents primal slumbers break,
The wondering red-man smiled and spake,
  They triumph o'er the flood!

Vast continent, its sides around,
Breaks with their fame, their deeds profound,
The distant nations catch the sound,
  Re-echo through the world;—
Breaks now the prophets' seventh seal,
The thrones of tyrants quake and reel,
Loud rolls great Freedom's anthem peal,
  Its banners high unfurled!

Improvement, culture, star the race,
Great wrongs of ages flee apace,
Proud Honor triumph's o'er Disgrace,
  Crumbles each guilty shrine!

Comes now the mighty, golden age,
Fills with new light Time's grandest page,
The mightiest themes mankind engage,
      Earth breaks with beams divine!

Hail, Pilgrim band! of high renown!
Your grateful sons with honor crown,
Your fame to ages passes down,
      Breaks with increasing light!
Long as yon sun shall rise and flame,
Posterity shall speak your name,
Tell the great deeds for which you came,
      In Glory's radiance bright!

Two hundred fifty years have flown,
They die not, live, remembered, known,
Their mighty deeds are brighter grown,
      We wreath with humble lay;
They of the sainted dead, sublime,
In triumph sleep, o'er Change and Time,
While centuries roll, and peal, and chime,
      They live in endless day!

26

The paths Time's Heaven-commissioned actors
    tread
Lie through vast, trackless deeps, with storms
    o'erspread,
Where lightnings blaze, where black'ning tem-
    pests shroud,
Where fall the heavens in pealing thunders
    loud,
Where earthquakes spring, where fiery whirl-
    winds rend,
Where mightiest powers their anger'd forces
    spend;
Breasting the mountain weight of tyrant woe,
They ope new crystal founts, whence life-tides
    flow;
Dissolve the starless glooms of terror's night,
Reveal new paths of sweet, returning light,
Sun-gemmed,—to dreaded foe fling gauntlet
    down,
Deck human brow with Truth's starred, pearl-
    bright crown;
Through rugged conflicts force their destined
    way
To victory, triumph, honor's glorious day!

Thus has the world, have ages, waxed and
 grown,
Great century wrongs, frauds, rapine, been o'er-
 thrown,
Imperial virtues, dawned and brightened,
 glowed,
Truth, foulness, scum, that deluged, overflowed,
The Augean filth, from Time's great realms
 been cast,
For sweet, returning bloom, life unsurpassed,
Been solved in every great, emergent hour,
Stamped with the seal of Heaven's approving
 power,
The mighty problems, on whose pivot lie
Man's commonweal, immortal Destiny!
All, all, who've felt the soul-enkindling flame,
Unknown, or high-entablatured with fame,
Great Pilgrim host, proud builders of mankind,
They live in man's fond memory enshrined;
We pay them homage, laud their deathless
 work,
All who, for man, through centuries have spoke,
Who, guides of power, with heart-impassioned
 zeal,

Have given their all, immortal good to seal!
Thus to the noble great, the faithful few,
Tribute unsought we pay the illustrious few,—
They who, through peril, wrath, through storms
    and flood,
Here sought the wilderness, for Freedom,
    God!
Who flung Truth's banner on a starless sky,
Begun great age of glory, ne'er to die,
The Mayflower band, immortal be their name,
Heaven's favored sons, eternal be their fame!

Stupendous hero toils of deep'ning Time come
    last,
Supernal deeds of glory, matchless, unsur-
    passed,
Great victories, trophies, triumphs, fruitage,
    honors grand,
Upbuilding power, rare products of each cul-
    tured land;
Man's panting spirit, struggling, undismayed,
    upbear,
Through night's long gloom, the splendors of
    the day to share,

Teach to the trembling race impassioned,
    wrung with grief,
That, stormy seas passed o'er, shall come the
    grand relief;
Through mountain billows piled, nature
    eclipsed, no sun,
Some grander period of the world shall be
    begun;
Through Time's great boundaries of utmost
    range to spread,
Great hero deeds, great acts of the immortal
    dead !
That 'tis through ignominies, sorrow, scorn,
    disgrace,
Man as he toils ascends to Glory's highest
    place,
Climbs through dissolving forces of this
    nether world,
Battling, to see his name on Fame's proud
    arch enrolled !
Would he the sovereign of the world's great
    heart still rise,
His name be onward wafted as each century
    flies ?

Then, 'mid vast promptings of the Present, let
    him learn
This mighty lesson, with its useful wisdom
    burn :—
Whate'er in Fates dark book, howe'er to
    man unkind,
Whate'er the prodigies of guilt passions un-
    bind,
Whate'er high Heaven inflicts, on sinning
    mortals due,
O'erwhelmed, oppressed, misguided, Time's
    drear pathway through,
Marked by convulsions, ruins, dark unfath-
    omed woe,
Huge miseries, while he perfection's joys
    would know ;
'Tis through great hero-martyr Faith, the
    toiling brain,
True generous sacrifice, comes man's imperi-
    al reign !
Great reign of intellect, of sovereign mind,
    warm with the Light,
Raying unmatched, bursting in God's supernal
    splendors bright,

Creative Power! at touch of whose enstarring, dazzling beam,
The monumented ages send their quenchless,
  bright'ning gleam,
Changing Time's blackened wastes, dark, woe-
  begone, dismantled world,
To paradise of joy, 'neath Freedom's starry
  flag unfurled!
Lo! 'twas through toil, through sacrifice of our
  great Pilgrim band,
Vast glowing destinies impend, await each rising land;
To travel onward, borne through greatening
  centuries of Time,
Earth's future mighty harvest-home, its gold-
  en fruit sublime!
That fruit's rare flower, its qualities, sweet
  healing, nurturing power,
Should Time approval come, may serve to
  charm some future hour,
Grace and adorn with meditations pure, serene, upright,
The sovereign Muse kindling anew for high
  exalting flight!

NOTES.

PART I.

Page 5th, five lines from the top,—" Two hundred fifty years ago." The Poem was written, as the preface indicates, from an incident in allusion to the two hundred and fiftieth anniversary of the landing of the Pilgrims.

Page 6th, eight lines from the top,—" They deep illume Time's ill-starred hour." It was ill-starred ; the Commonwealth had passed,—the Charleses, the Jameses, restored,—in authority,—the spirit of National Liberty resisted,—and all who might attempt the vindication of human rights, put under ban.

Page 7th, four lines from the bottom,—" Stud England's brow." Though vilely abused, and persecuted even unto death, Hume and Macauley affirm that the English Constitution derives all the liberty it contains from the efforts and labors of the Puritans, of which class the Pilgrims were most conspicuous.

Page 10th, ten lines from the bottom,—" Most glorious, gifted, of mankind." The Pilgrims were treated with such contempt and contumely by their cotemporaries, that multitudes have come to look upon them as narrow-minded, bigoted, and incapable of noble and magnanimous bearing,—whereas they were of the most cultivated, erudite, and polished society.

Page 20th, first line,—" To act some noble, generous part." Though the primary object of the Pilgrims was to get beyond the reach of the cruel oppressions of the motherland, yet from the first they had thoughts of laying foundations for improving the general human condition.

Page 30th, ten lines from the top,—" Time waxing darker evermore." The day of hope, for improving man's condition in Europe seemed to be over ; all was gigantic wrong.

Page 31st, three lines from the bottom,—" Votaries of prayer." The Pilgrims engaged in nothing without asking Heaven's guidance.

Page 32, eight lines from the top,—"Stern foes of war's dark, bloody fight." While the Pilgrims, as patriots, were ever ready to defend their country when assailed, they detested and abominated the bloody science of human butchery and slaughter, as inconsistent with the peaceful tendencies of Christ's Kingdom, for whose establishment they toiled.

Page 33, six lines from top,—"They give the nations grandest sight." It would be impossible, in heroic adventure, to hit upon anything in all the annals of the past, so truly grand and morally sublime as the voyage of the Pilgrims in the Mayflower for the new world.

Page 34, ten lines from top,—"Time's grandest destinies fulfil." Plato, in his Atlantis, imagined some happy region beyond the Western waters, where his dreams of a Republic might be realized. The Pilgrims executed what he only dreamed!

Page 35, seven lines from top,—"Martyrs of Truth, champions of Right." The Pilgrim doctrines of truth and right were the advanced thought of mankind,—little, new, has been discovered in morals since their day.

Page 35, six lines from bottom.—"The hills, from their deep, granite bed." That arm of land which sweeps away around Plymouth, ending at the Eastern extremity of Cape Cod, forms a harbor which breaks the wholesale fury of the ocean. Nature, sympathizing with the exiles in their hard lot, is here represented as she reposes on granite foundations, far in the interior as rising from her rocky base, rushing forward, settling down, as she goes, and flinging her arm around the sea-tossed bark to preserve it from foundering with its precious freight!

Page 36, five lines from bottom,—"Then pealed the mightiest bell of Time." In the lines which follow, the generous Past is recognized as in sympathy with the Pilgrims. It may seem, to some, a little fanciful, perhaps, but if the great and good lose nothing of their knowledge and aspiration as they pass to the Invisible, who can doubt that when great events occur, that set forward the destinies of man, they hover about and shed benedictions and pronounce blessings!

Page 39, nine lines from bottom,—"His mind transform, renew his heart." It was not governments, organizations, so much as individual man, that occupied the mind of the Pilgrims. In that respect they laid the foundations of a new era.

Page 42, bottom line,—"Lo! what events." The Western Hemisphere, our own civilization, our frame of Republican Government, constitute the grandest themes that now occupy the human mind, subordinate only to that of Atonement and Redemption.

Page 47, eight lines from bottom,—"Hark! 'tis the tramp of living men!" Never was there such an exodus of nations, to find the realization of dreams of human happiness, as that witnessed in the multitudes who come annually to find homes here.

Page 53, eight lines from top,—"Franklin disarms the bolted sky." The lines following are in allusion to an historical fact. It is said that Franklin had a laboratory in Philadelphia, where he passed wires zigzag around the sides, and when a thunder-tempest came over, if his wife was having a tea-party, he would invite them to the laboratory. Just as the cloud peered on the locality, he would suddenly close the window-shutters, send up his kite, when the electric agent would blaze and leap in zigzags and spirals, and fantastic movements, all around the room, when the women would shriek, and cry, and faint, to the no little amusement of the great sage.

Page 76, two lines from bottom,—"How Poesy, forever young." It is unquestionably the fact that for originality, freshness, force, fire, Homer lives, and will ever remain one of the greatest, grandest, and sublimest of the poetic lights. Milton has a nobler reach of objective imagination ; Shakspeare is by far a greater analyzer of the human heart and its emotions,—but Homer, when we consider the period in which he lived, his blindness, the paucity of help and aid he could receive through the promptings of predecessors or cotemporaries, must be considered as unrivaled in the whole line of time.

It can but be considered as truly wonderful that so early in the unfolding of the race so stupendous an example of what is most pleasing, select and divine, should have been given to man. That Poetry will still make progress we believe ;—there will be grander epics, lyrics, satire, ode, and sonnet ;—the race is not spent on any side of its development,—but that so early such an example should have appeared, is truly astonishing. For Poetry is the finished thought of life. It is the culmination of its choicest graces, excellencies. It is a divine spirit, lifting humanity to its loftiest moods, breathing intuitions, maxims, doctrines of supernal import, widening, enlarging its comprehension,—the reason, the judgment purging,—transforming beneath the outbursting, falling splendors of the imagination, until the immortal mind, kindling with the selectest fires of being, pours itself forth in sublimest harmonies of creative thought,—the quintessence of the True, the Beautiful, the Good,—destined to hold on its way forever, opening new paths of Light and Glory,—the finite within the perlieu of the Infinite,—the grandest approach of the human to the Limitless Supreme,—the farthest reach of flesh and blood, to discoveries of immortal and unerring vision. But great, sublime, as is its province, Homer, in his unequaled imagery, —his imaginative, prophetic glances,—the fertility, richness, of his ideas, is as wonderful to the cultivated and appreciative of after ages as he possibly could have been to cotemporaries,—for that which is poetry never dies. The same may be said of all the great bards that have charmed, enlightened and improved the race. Shakspeare and Milton can never die so long as anything truly generous, noble, sublime, continues to sway and control the human mind.

Pages 77, 78 and 79,—Plato, Demosthenes and Cicero, were their names blotted from human record, much that warms, thrills, instructs the succeeding generations, would be blotted out !

Page 98, first line at the top,—"Man, man alone waxes supreme." The great distinction between the recent modern and ancient civilizations, consists in the prominence given to individual man above corporate entities—systems of general import.

Page 101, eight lines from the top,—"Infernal witchcraft, horror's tale." That a strange delusion on the subject of witches, and being bewitched, occurred in the early colonial history, is notable, yet no more singular than in other instances.

Thirteenth line,—" The prudeless Quaker." It is often maintained that the Pilgrims abused the Quakers,—while history attests that all the punishment they received was for having violated decency, by going naked, in instances, into public assemblies.

Page 108, ten lines from the bottom,—"A form Herculean in might." It is hoped the following characterization of the Pilgrims may not seem overwrought,— and will not, the author thinks, when the Pilgrims are compared with other material that enters into the compound of human civilization.

PART II.

Page 121, two lines from the bottom,—" Their influence lives." This Second Part of the work is but a continuation of the First, with specific references to certain characteristic features of Pilgrim life,—home, country, &c.,—of Pilgrim influence under the guidance of Christian faith.

Page 130, eight lines from the top,—" On rock of adamant they tower." The Pilgrims, with whatever might be objected as drawbacks upon their life and char- acter, are everywhere recognized as a crowning force in society, while the colonial settlements arising, based on schemes of speculation, in influence dwindle, and are destitute of grand results. The author might as well state in a word, which will have appropriateness to most of the Second Part, his desire to vindicate Christian faith as one of the grandest elements in the building of human society, signally illustrated in the case of the Pilgrims.

Page 136,—" They come to build new, sweet, sweet home." The Pilgrim idea of home,—the family,—its purity is what we must cherish,—if we desire our institu- tions of civil government to be permanent.

Page 161, four lines from the top,—" Country, it stars through course of Time." The eulogiums bestowed on Country, it is hoped, will not be looked upon otherwise than as just tribute to the noble conceptions and unswerving patriotism of the found- ers of this country.

Page 186, nine lines from the bottom,—" Vast heights ascended." The popular error has been that the Pilgrims, from their orthodoxy, were necessarily narrow, exclusive, bigoted, dogmatic, and over-precise. The fact is, they were the only truly liberal men of their time. Truth, when received in true proportions, symmetrizes, ennobles mind.

Page 200, eleven lines from the bottom,—" And breaks glad morn of Europe's day." The Hungarians, in the thirteenth century of the Christian era, maintained the Faith against the barbarian Turks and Tartar hordes from Asia. [See Gibbons, Vol. VI.]

Page 205, eleven lines from bottom,—" Th' apocalyptic Anti-Christ." The rise and progress of Papacy in Modern Europe, has been more ominous in evil, than foul- est oppressions of civil tyrants.

Page 208, top line,—" See Luther, light on darkness pour." Martin Luther has been one of the greatest of civil, as well as moral, benefactors of the race. He revolutionized human society, and started it on its true foundations, Faith in God !

Page 241, four lines from bottom,—" Would you a power supremely great." It is an acknowledged fact that the ancient civilizations fell, for want of some element of permanence.

Page 244, four lines from top,—" A Midas-wand." It was the long search of ancient philosophy to find something whose transmuting touch should turn all things to gold. What was its vain search, Christianity more than supplies. Though it may not directly create material wealth, fortune, it lays the foundations of society in such a manner that, while every virtue finds true support, through the order and confidence it everywhere inspires among mankind, all material successes are amazingly enhanced.

Page 245, two lines from bottom,—" It whispers clouds shall pass away." There is nothing that gives such luster, stability, and true confidence to the young, as Faith.

Page 246, eleven lines from bottom,—" Far down the steep of wreathless time." The mightiest poets have been vastly diffident of their ability to instruct and delight, which are the true functions of poetry.

Page 248, top line,—" Assured that sorrow points the way." Faith, Christianity, has ever been, and will continue to be, the crowning solace of the ills of mediocrity and distressing poverty.

Page 249, four lines from bottom,—" Two blended hearts, by Love made one." An allusion to a youthful hero in the wars of Alfred, betrothed to a young princess of exquisite beauty and genius.

Page 255, seven lines from bottom,—" Base infidels, believing men." It is notorious that scoffers and revilers of Christianity, when overtaken by unusual accidents or calamities, are oftenest found ready to implore deliverance by some supernal Power. The Deity they hate, they involuntarily confess.

Page 257, ten lines from bottom,—" Mysterious paths unknown, pursue." Death, when made direct object of thought, even to Christian believers, comes clad in terrors. Faith, however, is its supreme antidote. Christ has conquered Death. Though it has a period, it is put in bounds,—and is doomed, dragged at the chariot wheels of Christ's triumph.

Page 262, eleven lines from bottom,—" Sublimer grows each setting sun." Whatever theories may be broached, as a fact in history and Providence, abundantly authenticated by all worth observation, the Christian system strikes deeper and deeper its roots.

Page 264, nine lines from bottom,—" All battle-fields grow holy ground." The spirit of Christianity is opposed to bloodshed and oppressive wars. Wherever tyrants impose chains, it calls, yea, inspires men of every age to sunder them, and assert their true liberties.